Seattle
BREWS

Seattle BREWS

The Insider's Guide to Neighborhood Alehouses, Brewpubs, and Bars

BY BART BECKER

Alaska Northwest Books™
Anchorage • Seattle

Library of Congress Cataloging-in-Publication Data
Becker, Bart, 1950–
    Seattle brews : the insider's guide to neighborhood alehouses,
  brewpubs, and bars / by Bart Becker.
        p.   cm.
    Includes index.
    ISBN 0-88240-425-3
    1. Hotels, taverns, etc.—Washington (State)—Seattle—Guidebooks.
    2. Breweries—Washington (State)—Seattle—Guidebooks.   3. Beer.
    I. Title.
    TX950.53.B43   1992
    641.2'3'09797772—dc20   92-18587
                                                                CIP

Project editor: Ellen Wheat
Editors: Ina Chang, Carolyn Smith
Cover and book design: Elizabeth Watson
Cover illustration: David L. Berger
Illustrations of alehouse, brewpub, and bar logos are reproduced courtesy
of those business establishments.

Recipe credits. The author has collected some of his favorite beer recipes from a variety of
sources: "Classic Beer Cheese" (p. 143) and "Trout in Beer" (p. 151) are from *Great
Cooking with Beer* by Jack Erickson, © 1989; reprinted by permission of Red Brick Press.
"Beer and Onion Soup" (p. 148) is from *The Vegetarian Epicure, Book Two* by Anna Thomas,
© by Anna Thomas and Julie Maas; reprinted by permission of Alfred A. Knopf, Inc. "Beer-
Steamed Clams" (p. 150) is taken from *Beer Cuisine: A Cookbook for Beer Lovers,* © 1991 by
Jay Harlow; reprinted by permission of Harlow & Ratner (distributed by Publishers Group
West). "Ale Flip," "Burton Soda," and "Island Grog" are from *The Association of Brewers'
Dictionary of Beer and Brewing,* compiled by Carl Forget.

Alaska Northwest Books™
A division of GTE Discovery Publications, Inc.
22026 20th Avenue S. E.
Bothell, WA 98021

Printed in U.S.A.

ACKNOWLEDGMENTS

Drinking beer is easy, but writing a book about it is not. A lot of people deserve thanks for their help and guidance. My wife, Enid, was always ready to join me for a night-on-the-town research excursion, and was equally cheerful about spending evenings at home while I wrote the book. I have to mention the great beer makers of Seattle—Paul Shipman at Redhook, Mike Hale at Hale's Ales, Charles Finkel at Pike Place, George Hancock at Maritime, and Bert Grant at Grant's—all of whom were convivial people and generous with their time. Beyond that, I've enjoyed the erudite companionship of many gourmet-beer drinking buddies. I have had the privilege and pleasure of buying a beer for some choice human beings, and even better, I've had some of them buy a beer for me. I appreciated all the free advice. And then the real work began, so I also have to hoist a pint to the world's greatest editors: Marlene Blessing, Ellen Wheat, Carolyn Smith, and Ina Chang.

CONTENTS

The Bettmann Archive

"YOU'LL NEVER MISS THE WATER

WINTERHOOK™
■■CHRISTMAS ALE■■

139 When Beer Meets Food

161 Other Regional Brewpubs and Microbreweries

169 Organizations, Publications, and Events

172 More Reading About Brews

173 Index

The Best Place in

AMERICA

to Drink Beer

THE REDHOOK ALE BREWERY · SEATTLE, WASHINGTON™

§eattle is the best place in America to drink beer. No other place in the nation boasts more variety and better quality in microbrewery beers. Seattle aficionados can choose from dozens of delicious, complex ales made by small hometown breweries

9

"In the Northwest, we have the most sophisticated beer consumer in the country. We're looking at a new Munich here in terms of a beer culture in America."
—Jim McConnaughey, *Cascade Beer News*

such as Redhook, Hale's, Maritime, and Pike Place. Pour in the brews from nearby Washington and Oregon breweries, such as Grant's, Thomas Kemper, Pyramid, Full Sail, Rogue, and Black Butte, and beer drinking here is a real mouthful.

Not only are these beers flavorful and distinctive, but they are fairly easy to find. Redhook, the largest of the small breweries, distributes its beers to 500 Seattle taverns. Quite a few bars and restaurants specialize in high-quality brews, and almost every grocery store carries a few microbrews.

Microbrews are made by small breweries, sometimes one-person operations—that's where the prefix "micro" comes from. Even the largest of these independent breweries—some produce a substantial

50,000 barrels a year—are just a drop in Anheuser-Busch's bucket.

Almost all of the Seattle microbreweries specialize in ale, for a couple of reasons. First, ale is easier for a small brewery to make than lager, the other main style. (Lager is the lighter type of beer made by major breweries, typified by Budweiser and Miller.) Second, and more important to the drinker, ale-brewing produces a richer variety of complex tastes.

People in the craft-brewing business tend to use the terms "beer," "brew," "microbrew," and "ale" interchangeably. There are differences, of course. In general, "beer" is an all-encompassing term that also covers the major American beers. But for the most part, when "beer" is used in this book, it refers to the distinctive product of microbreweries, not the beer produced by conglomerate breweries.

There is much to learn, savor, and contemplate about craft beer. But even so, you don't have to *know* a lot to truly enjoy drinking a beer. A little know-how can enhance the experience, but beer drinking is foremost a social activity and it shouldn't be turned into a seminar. Beer is for everybody. And great beer is poetry, not science.

Fortunately, beer has no sacrosanct vintages. Everybody has different tastes, and the variety of brews available in the Northwest provides something for just about everyone. I consider myself a fairly typical Northwest beer drinker in that I became an enthusiast by trying different brews over time. Now, depending on my mood or the setting, I may order a refreshing wheat beer or a pale ale, but my true favorites are the heavier and darker ales, such as porter and some of the less-sweet stouts. Give me a

When Stephen Morris, author of *The Great Beer Trek*, surveyed 200 beer experts about the best places in America to drink beer, Seattle was the most frequently named city.

Moss Bay Irish Stout, a Maritime Navigator, or a Black Butte and I am in heaven.

My own evolution as a beer drinker parallels the development of microbrewing as an industry. The 1980s were the right time for the microbrew revolution to start. Consumers showed a willingness to pay a little more for a higher quality product. This was true for food—whether a thick-crusted loaf of peasant bread, a tasty ripe tomato, a distinctive regional wine, or a high-octane cup of espresso. It was no surprise that consumers also sought more flavor, character, and variety in their beers. As the number of sophisticated beer drinkers grew, so did the market for fine beer, and what had once been a subculture became a thriving industry.

In the 1990s, consumers are pursuing a healthier, more moderate lifestyle, and craft beer fits right in. A bottle of beer has about 150 calories. A normal, active person is not going to grow a beer belly as a result of drinking a few glasses of ale. Beer is also a sensible choice for people who are watching their alcohol intake. Most people recognize that it's a bad idea to drink too much, and the idea of microbrews is *not* to get bombed. Rather, it is to savor a beer or two in a convivial environment. Even the nature of microbrews themselves mitigates overconsumption: they're expensive and they're filling.

If the '80s and '90s are the right time for the microbrewing boom, Seattle is the right place. Seattleites delight in choosing to stand apart from the rest of mainstream American taste. We are idiosyncratic in our politics, our social mores, our

"Think Globally, Drink Locally."
—Hale's Ales motto

leisure pursuits, our habits, our outlook on life. Even our cool, moist climate is a complement to the full-bodied and robust ales. So local microbreweries fit right in. They make good beer, they're right around the corner, and they're a part of our good life.

"Did you ever taste beer?" "I had a sip of it once," said the small servant. "Here's a state of things!" cried Mr. Swiveller. "She *never* tasted it—it can't be tasted in a sip!" —Charles Dickens, *The Old Curiosity Shop*

**"In Heaven there is no beer,/That's why we drink it here."
—American drinking song**

Part of the microbrew mentality, and part of the reason for this book, is the desire to once again make food a central element of our social lives. So much of our contemporary lifestyle—fast-food restaurants, microwave meals—puts convenience before pleasure; we need more opportunities to celebrate the experience of food and drink in an atmosphere that, in beer writer Jack Erickson's words, "nourishes the soul as much as it does the body."

Not to state the obvious, but beer drinking is a *leisure* activity. It's a mental-health break. It's a glorious waste of time, not a gainful pursuit. So a drinking establishment should create a comfortable atmosphere somewhere between that of a lazy riverbank and that of a warm living room. A pleasant quaffing spot should have personality. It should be individualistic, even idiosyncratic. A good name helps, though it's no guarantee of a good drinking environment. Many of the best places to drink beer in Seattle are entirely wholesome, from fine restaurants to cheerful brewpubs. Some are smoke-free. But some of the *other* best places to drink beer are smoky and worn. What these drinkeries have in common is that they all care about beer and are all concerned with making customers happy, not just with making money fly out of their billfolds.

I like them all.

A Brief
HISTORY
of Beer

The Bettmann Archive

We know that beer has been around for about 8,000 years, based on archaeological artifacts from Mesopotamia. That country's Queen Shu-Bad (sounds like a rap singer) even sipped her brew through a golden straw. Some scientists actually think that early nomads made the switch

Saint Arnou is
the patron saint
of brewers. He
was born in 580
in the old French
diocese of Toul,
north of Nancy,
and became
Bishop of Metz.
After his death in
640, when his
body was being
ceremoniously
carried from St.
Mont to Metz, a
loaves-and-fishes-
style miracle
took place in a
town called
Champigneulles.
The tired
entourage
stopped for a
rest and a drink.
There was only
one mug of beer
to be shared, but
the mug never
went dry and
everyone was
refreshed.

to primitive agriculture for the specific purpose of growing grains from which to make beer, although more orthodox science suggests bread. In any event, the first beer was valuable as food; its role as intoxicant was secondary.

Beer Through the Ages

Beer and brewing occasionally flavor the study of history. A clay tablet inscribed in Babylonia around 6000 B.C. depicts the preparation of beer for sacrificial purposes. By 4000 B.C., the Babylonians were making 16 different types of beer from barley, wheat, and honey. Bittering agents (to add character to the taste and a degree of shelf life) have been used in beer making since 3000 B.C. Beer was common in China by about 2300 B.C. And in the Pharaohs' Egypt, a beer called *hek* was brewed from partially baked bread made of germinated barley. The Greeks and Romans learned brewing from the Egyptians. (The Greek historian Herodotus wrote a treatise on beer in 460 B.C.)

Brewing was also common among the barbarian tribes of Europe, who made drinks from wheat or barley and sweetened them with honey. In premedieval Europe, wherever there was no significant viticulture, beer or beerlike beverages (such as barley wine) were an important part of the culture.

In the early medieval period, home brewing contributed to better health because water supplies were always chancy, and often dangerous; fermentation destroyed many harmful micro-organisms, so people of all ages (including little kids) drank beer.

Because exotic flavorings such as herbs and date juice were used, most early beers would taste strange

It is said that
Queen Elizabeth I
could drink any
of her suitors
under the
refectory table,
and ladies of her
court received an
allowance of two
gallons of beer a
day. This was
also the age of
New World
exploration,
colonization, and
piracy. Ships
sailed with a
supply of beer.
Beer was
relatively free
from
contamination,
offered some
sustenance, and
may even have
helped fend off
scurvy.

to modern drinkers. But a brew similar to what we
drink today could certainly have been found in parts
of Europe by the Middle Ages. Beer as we know it
began with the acceptance of hops as the dominant
flavoring agent. Hops provide the characteristic
bitterness that makes beer refreshing. Beers
sweetened with honey or dates may have been tasty,
but they cannot have been very thirst-quenching.
Throughout the Middle Ages, hop-flavored beer
gained in popularity—in part, perhaps, because hops
also act as a natural preservative.

The earliest record of hops used in beer is in the
Physica Sacia of 1079 by the Abbess Hildegard of
Rupertsberg, which says, "If one intends to make beer
from oats, it is prepared with hops, but is boiled with
grug, and mostly with ash leaves." Most of us have
tasted the occasional modern beer characterized by
grug and ash leaves, so we can see the direct lineage.
Actually, grug probably meant herbs.

By the 11th century, the beer trade was firmly in
the hands of the clergy. Monasteries developed a

"A delicious
remedy against
death—half
an onion in
beer foam."
—Egyptian
medical manual,
1600 B.C.

highly refined brewing tradition, often hand-in-hand with baking.

Interestingly, British ales, now so aggressively hopped, were made without benefit of the bitter ingredient until about 1500, when Flemish immigrants introduced the taste for hops. Ales began to proliferate. Porter, a more robust kind of ale, was devised around 1722, followed by the even heartier stout.

With the coming of the Reformation and the weakening of the Church of Rome in England and Northern Europe, some monasteries were stripped of their beermaking function. This made room for the entrepreneurial, commercial brewer—one more step

on the road to modern beer.

Until the 19th century, lager beers (the sparkling, refreshing kind of beer now typified by commercial American brands) were rare, but could be found in Bavaria (Germany) and Bohemia (Czechoslovakia). These beers had to be fermented at a low temperature, then stored for weeks in a cool, dark place (the German word *lagern* means "to store"). In short, this was a perfect beer to brew in a Bavarian cave, but hardly anyplace else. In the 1800s, industrial refrigeration made large-scale lager production possible. Lager was clearer than ale, it kept better, and it even had a different taste—lighter and less bitter. Today, lager is often called pilsner, after the town of Pilsen, Bohemia, where a famous brand called Pilsner Urquell was first brewed in 1842. It was very much like today's Michelob. This lively, foaming beer was something new, and more palatable to many people.

Despite the ascendancy of pilsner, there was ongoing resistance to lager and staunch loyalty to ale in the British Isles, in certain German cities, and in Belgium.

Beer in America

The Incas were making corn-based beer centuries before Europeans arrived in the Americas. When the Spanish conquistadors moved north into Navajo country in what is now the southwestern United States, the Native Americans were drinking *chica,* a beer made from maize. And on the other side of the

"We could not now take time for further searche or consideration: our victuals being much spente, especially our beere."
—Logbook of the *Mayflower,* December 19, 1620

"To make Small Beer—Take a large Siffer full of Bran Hops to your taste.—Boil these 3 hours. Then strain out 30 Gall'ns into a Cooler. Put in 3 Gall'ns Molasses while the Beer is Scalding hot or rather draw the Molasses into the Cooler & Strain the Beer on it while boiling Hot. Let this stand till it is little more than Blood Warm.

Continued on next page

continent, at the forlorn Roanoke Island colony, settled in 1585 under the leadership of Sir Walter Raleigh, an account by one of the English settlers reported: "Wee made of the same in the countrey some mault, whereof was brued as good ale as was to be desired."

Dutch settlers were making beer in New Amsterdam (in what is now New York) before the arrival of the *Mayflower* in 1620. Two men named Block and Christiansen set up a brewery there in

1612, and a decade later another Dutchman named Peter Minuit established a public brewery near today's Wall Street.

But until the 19th century, most beer was brewed in the tavern or at home. Because there was no mechanical refrigeration, beer was generally served at a warmer temperature than we are used to today. Comparisons with Northwest microbrews would not be unreasonable, although the 18th-century beers were certainly inferior in clarity and stability to the contemporary product.

Bottled beer was not unknown, but it tended to spoil easily. (Most households had a beer pail that they filled at the neighborhood tavern.) By the mid-1880s, however, the public demand for beer led to better bottling. The typical beer bottle of that period was green, held a quart, and had a cork. Canned beer wasn't introduced until the 1930s.

The wave of pilsner-drinking German and Czech immigrants in the 1800s led to the establishment of breweries by such men as Joseph Schlitz and August Busch, who became beer barons. As their beers became more widely distributed, the taste became more and more diluted. By the post-World War II era, Americans wanted their beer to complement the rest of their lifestyle: white bread, golfing president, TV dinners. A can of Falstaff fit right in. The evolution of bottling and packaging—resulting in the six-pack— made beer even handier to drink, but the flavor suffered.

Even then, the country had a healthy local and regional brewing scene. Almost every town had its local beer: Iron City in Pittsburgh, Pickett in Dubuque, Grain Belt in Minneapolis. In the Northwest, Rainier

"Then put in a quart of Yeast. If the Weather is very Cold cover it over with a Blanket & let it Work in the Cooler 24 hours. Then put it into the Cask—leave the Bung open till it is almost done Working— Bottle it that day a Week from the day it was Brewed."
—George Washington's home recipe

In 1638, William Penn built the first brewery in Pennsylvania.

and Olympia had status as tasty local brews. Even if most of the regional favorites aspired to the same aesthetic standards as the mass-produced national beers, they were a source of local pride. A few still struggle on proudly, but most have been either driven out of business or swallowed up by the larger companies. Seattle's Rainier Brewery is fairly typical. It has retained its name, but is now owned by the G. Heileman brewing conglomerate.

This trend has only accelerated over the past few decades. Most grocery-store coolers are filled with a mix of commercial light beers and high-potency malt liquors. Beer ads on television are filled with hot cars, sexy (and often sexist) situations, and thinly veiled endorsements of overconsumption. It appears that the target audience for most American commercial beer is a young adult with arrested emotional development and an unsophisticated palate. This entire scenario is what the microbrew revolution is reacting against.

Early Seattle Breweries

Washington has had 138 breweries over the years, most of them in Seattle, according to the book *Brewed in the Pacific Northwest* by Gary and Gloria Meier. Most Seattle breweries boomed from the 1870s until state prohibition in 1916. The undisputed king was Andrew Hemrich, whose Seattle Brewing & Malting Company (now Rainier Brewing) simply bought up most potential challengers.

The first brewery in Seattle was the Washington Brewery at Fourth and Yesler, which began making beer, porter, and cream ale in 1864 and operated under a number of different owners until 1888.

In 1865, the North Pacific Brewery opened at First and Columbia. It changed hands and moved several times, and was eventually bought by the Hemrich family in 1897. They operated it at Yale and Republican until 1916.

The Claussen-Sweeney Brewing Company, a large brewery in Georgetown near present-day Boeing Field, opened in 1884. Albert Braun Brewing Association, makers of Columbia Beer, set up shop in 1890. In 1893, both breweries merged with Andrew Hemrich's Bay View Brewery, forming Seattle Brewing & Malting Company.

Brewed in the Pacific Northwest lists many other short-lived Seattle breweries: Cantierri Brewery, 1874–75; Julius Weigert Brewing Company, Lake Union, 1889–90; West & Company (later renamed Seattle Ale and Porter Company, and still later American Brewing Company), Westlake and Galer, 1899-1903; Standard Brewing Company, 3255 21st Avenue West, 1901 (bought out by Hemrich); Spellmire–West Brewing Company (renamed Washington Brewing Company in 1913), 1320 Almy Street, 1905–1916; Independent Brewing Company, Eighth Avenue South and Pacific, 1902–1916; Apex Brewing Company (a Hemrich subsidiary), Ninth Avenue South (now Airport Way) and Hanford, 1933–37; Horluck Brewing Company, 606 Westlake Avenue, opened in 1934, absorbed by Emil Sick's company in 1939, closed in 1957; Pilsener Brewing Company, 548 First Avenue South, 1934–35; Western Brewing Company (a Hemrich subsidiary), 5225 East Marginal Way, 1934–40; Elmer E. Hemrich Brewery Company (Elmer was nephew of Andrew Hemrich; the brewery was later renamed Gold Seal), 1935–40.

Charles II, in his Tippling Act, said the inn should be "a place for the receipt, relief, lodging of wayfaring people; it is not meant for the entertaining and harboring of lewd and idle people to spend and consume their time and money in lewd and idle manner."

Rainier Beer

"For a quart of
ale is a dish for
a king."
—William
Shakespeare,
A Winter's Tale

Andrew Hemrich learned the brewer's trade at his father's brewery in Alma, Wisconsin, before moving to Seattle and opening Bay View Brewery in 1883. In 1893 Hemrich's brewery merged with two other local breweries, resulting in the giant Seattle Brewing & Malting Company. This company, operated by Hemrich and several of his brothers, continued to grow through the turn of the century. Through all the expansion, Rainier Beer was the principal label. The Rainier slogan was "There's new vigor and strength in every drop."

By 1914, Seattle Brewing & Malting was the largest industrial enterprise in Washington and the sixth largest brewery in the United States. (At 6004 Airport Way South, in Georgetown, you can still find massive brick buildings with signs proclaiming "Brew House" and "Malt House.") In 1916, state prohibition hit. The Hemrich Brothers sold the Rainier name to a California company and went into other businesses. With Repeal in 1933, the Hemrichs reopened their brewery and began making Apex beer. In 1935, they sold the operation to Fritz and Emil Sick.

The Sicks built a new facility, the current Rainier complex at 3100 Airport Way South, and began brewing Rheinlander and Highlander beers. In 1938, they repurchased the Rainier brand name, and Rainier Beer once again became the company's premier product. To celebrate, Emil Sick bought the Seattle Indians baseball team, renamed them the Rainiers, and installed them in a new field, Sick's Stadium in the Rainier Valley.

In 1957, Emil Sick changed the name of Seattle Brewing & Malting Company to Sicks' Rainier

Brewing Company. After his death in 1964, Molson Breweries of Canada bought a majority share of the brewery. In 1977, G. Heileman Brewing Company bought the company and in 1987, Bond Corporation Holdings of Australia acquired Heileman.

Rainier, of course, is anything but a microbrewery, but it is a major Seattle institution. At one time, Rainier offered the ultimate brewing tour—free beer and lunch for a nickel—and you didn't even have to tour the plant to qualify. No such luck anymore, but the brewery does offer tours on weekday afternoons.

"As he brews, so shall he drink."
—Ben Jonson,
Every Man Out of His Humour

The Microbrewery Boom

The stage was set for the 1980s microbrew boom a decade earlier, when sales of imported beer in the United States began to take off. As more Americans became interested in gourmet food and wine, they also began to notice flavorful European beers. Ethnic restaurants helped spur interest in imported beers, and the added cachet of imports made beer drinking more acceptable in fine restaurants.

Microbrew lore traces the American beer renaissance to Jack McAuliffe, who became enamored of malty Scottish ales while stationed with the U.S. Navy in Scotland. When he returned to the United States he began homebrewing and eventually opened the New Albion Brewing Company in Sonoma, California, in 1977. The beer was good, but the business was shaky; New Albion folded in 1983.

The best place to drink beer is at home. Or on a river bank, if the fish don't bother you.
—American folk saying

Nevertheless, once the keg was tapped, there was no stopping the flow, and other beer connoisseurs soon followed in McAuliffe's footsteps. Among the early microbreweries was San Francisco's Anchor Steam. It had been failing, but was revived by new owners in the late 1960s and really took off in the mid-1970s. Before long, the first brewpubs—establishments serving draft beer brewed right on the premises—began to appear. Brewpub pioneer Bill Owens, proprietor of Buffalo Bill's Brewery and Brew Pub in Hayward, California, credits the popularity of brewpubs such as his to one simple factor: "It's the beer," he says. "It's unpasteurized and unfiltered. It has legs; it has taste. By legs I mean it'll stand up and walk out of the glass."

The microbrewery industry is still growing. Little one-person operations are still popping up out of the homebrewing subculture. A handful survive, and a

"YOU'LL NEVER MISS THE WATER

12 FL.OZ. 355 ML.

Grant's

SCOTTISH ALE

BRAND

A rich Real ale, styled after the traditional premium brews of Scotland.

Contains only: pure water, pure yeast, premium barley malt and the finest Cascade hops.

"I have fed purely upon ale; I have eat my ale, and I always sleep upon ale."
—George Farquhar, *The Beaux' Stratagem*

few even flourish. At the other end of the spectrum, some of the bigger "small" breweries, such as Seattle's Redhook, are expanding.

Seattle's craft-brewing movement began in 1982, when two breweries opened almost simultaneously. Veteran beermaker Bert Grant began producing the assertively hopped Grant's Scottish Ale at his Yakima Brewing & Malting Company, and the new Redhook Brewery began production in Seattle. Redhook's early attempts at making fruity, Belgian-style ale are still remembered in Seattle beer circles. As Redhook president Paul Shipman once put it, "The city was extremely polite while we figured out how to make beer." In May 1984, Redhook introduced Ballard Bitter, which became one of the best-selling microbrews in the region and in effect saved the brewery. Redhook also straightened out the taste of Redhook Ale itself, and began brewing the fine Blackhook Porter.

An inscription on
a clay goblet
dating back to
the Gallo–Roman
wars reads,
"Cervesariis
feliciter." In
English: "Long
live the
beermakers."

Hale's Ales opened in Colville, north of Spokane, in 1983. The next year, more microbreweries opened in the Northwest, including Hart Brewing in Kalama (Pyramid Pale Ale) and Kemper Brewing in Poulsbo on the Kitsap Peninsula (Thomas Kemper Ale).

By this time, microbrews had become quite a fad, and beer tastings, festivals, and promotions were being held all over the state. In 1985, Seattle restaurateur Mick McHugh sponsored an expedition of Seattle-area brewers to the Great British Beer Festival, where Grant's, Hale's, Redhook, and Pyramid ales garnered attention. Although much of the novelty of that period has worn off, it is now de rigeur for Seattle bars to have at least a few microbrews on tap. More and more alehouses are opening up specifically to serve the beer cognoscenti, and a number of brewpubs have opened next to small craft breweries.

At one time, the term "microbrewery" meant a brewery that produced fewer than 10,000 barrels of beer annually (one barrel equals 31 gallons). Breweries such as Redhook and California's Sierra Nevada and Anchor have exceeded this volume, but the terms are not so narrowly defined anymore and any "boutique" or "cottage" brewery qualifies. Seattle beer writer Vince Cottone uses the handy term "true beer"—contrasted with mass-produced "industrial beer"—to define the "ideal, uncompromising beer, beer that's hand-made locally in small batches using quality natural ingredients, served on draft fresh and unpasteurized." Happily enough for Northwest brewers, this is what more and more drinkers want.

How
BEER
is Made

*A*ll vegetable matter, given sufficient moisture, appropriate temperature range, and the proper yeasts, will undergo some kind of decomposition or fermentation. So it would not be entirely disingenuous to say that beer more or less makes itself, as long as

**Composition
of beer (12 fluid
ounces):
Water 92%
Protein 1.1 g
Fat 0.0 g
Carbohydrate
14 g
Measurable
amounts of
calcium, sodium,
thiamine,
riboflavin, niacin.
—Source: U.S.
Department of
Agriculture**

somebody keeps an eye on it.

In the basic ale-brewing process, malted barley is crushed, mashed with hot (150° F) water, and filtered to produce a liquid called wort (pronounced "wert"). The wort is boiled, hops are added, the wort is cooled, yeast is added, the brew ferments, and finally the finished ale goes into kegs or bottles. The whole process takes anywhere from a week to a month, depending on how long the beer sits for "conditioning." Ales are made with top-fermenting yeast, which rises to the top of the fermentation tank once it's done taking care of business. Ales have a shorter, hotter fermentation period than bottom-fermenting lagers.

Beer can actually be made from any cereal grain—barley, corn, wheat, rice, oats, or rye. The grain contributes color, sweetness, body, and nutrients, but most important, it supplies the starch that is converted into sugar. The sugar, in turn, is transformed into alcohol during fermentation. Barley is by far the best grain for making beer because it provides the fullest body and the richest, most invitingly complex bouquet and flavor. Even so-called wheat beer is about 60 percent barley and 40 percent wheat. It is the smell of malted barley that assails you when you pass a brewery.

Since beer is about 90 percent water, the quality of the water affects the quality of the beer. That's why beer commercials are soaked through with any number of icy mountain streams. Most breweries, however, are not located in the Land of Sky Blue Waters, so they use plain old tap water.

The most important flavoring element is the hops, which are added in the middle of the brewing process. Hops provide the characteristic dry bitterness that we recognize as beer flavor. The key to good beer is the right combination of sweetness from barley and bitterness from hops. The hop plant, *Humulus lupulus,* is a

A 1516 German law called *Reinheitsgebot* mandated that beer be made from just four ingredients: malted barley, hops, yeast, and water.

The world's five most celebrated hop-growing regions are Bohemia in Czechoslovakia, Bavaria in Germany, Kent in England, Tasmania in Australia, and the Yakima Valley in Washington state.

climbing vine, and the female hop flower—a small, yellowish green, soft-leaved "pine cone" about an inch long—is used in beer. The tangy hops balance the natural sweetness of barley malt and pique the appetite. Some beer aficionados like their drink well-hopped. Beer writer Terry Foster has coined the term "lupomaniac" to describe the person who thinks that beer can never be too hoppy.

The brewing process is basically the same for ale and for lager. The early stages of brewing—mashing, boiling, and hopping—take only a few hours. The beer is then transferred to fermentation tanks, where yeast is added to convert the sugars to alcohol. (In winemaking, the yeast comes from the grape skins; in beermaking, it has to be added.) Yeast also contributes to the flavor and aroma of the beer. The brew sits in the fermentation tank for between four days and a week or so. The volatile mixture begins to work itself into a frenzy and produces a thick, foamy head. Once fermentation is completed, the top-fermenting yeast is "harvested"—literally scooped off the top. In lager brewing, the yeast sinks to the bottom.

The beer is then usually filtered and transferred into conditioning or aging tanks, where it sits for

anywhere from a week to a month. Then it's "racked" (funneled into kegs) or bottled. Before bottling, commercial beer is usually filtered or pasteurized, which gives it more staying power but mutes the taste. Indeed, some ales are encouraged to continue fermenting in the bottle or cask; these are called "cask-conditioned" or "bottle-aged" beers.

Types of Beer: Terms and Terminology

ALE

Ale, the traditional drink of the British Isles, is the type of beer made by most microbrewers and is the dominant Northwest style. Ale is easier for small brewers to make, since it uses a yeast that is effective at warm temperatures and that rises to the surface, where it can be skimmed off and used again in the next batch of beer.

Ale is a complex drink, with a more pronounced hop flavor than lager. It also tastes more bitter or tart, is generally more full-bodied, and often has a higher alcoholic content than lager. It's more of a mouthful. Ales are made more for savoring than for refreshment, although a cool ale is certainly an invigorating drink. Within any category of ale, there are differences from brewery to brewery. And porter and stout are both types of ale. The following are some common types of ale.

Bitter Ale. "Bitter" is the everyday draft beer of the British Isles. The color covers a range from amber to mahogany. The alcohol content is moderate. This beer is typically malty, full-bodied, and aromatic. It is always highly hopped and often extremely bitter, hence the name.

Pale Ale. Don't mistake this meaty brew for light beer. It is the bottled equivalent of bitter ale. It's often not even pale in color; it's called "pale" to contrast it with the blackish stouts and porters. A high degree of carbonation is acceptable in the bottled version, which sometimes also has a more pronounced malt flavor. The label India Pale Ale denotes a high-quality pale ale.

Porter. "Pours like mud," they say happily of this bittersweet beverage. Porter is an almost-black brew with a sudsy head. It is made with roasted, caramelized malt, which accounts for the color. It is darker, thicker, richer, and heavier than traditional ale, has a medium to medium-high alcohol content, and can range from quite bitter to mild and sweet. The name derives from its popularity among laborers—the porters—in 18th-century London markets.

Stout. Once porter became popular, British brewers started making a stout porter, an even darker, richer, creamier, maltier, sweeter, hoppier, and more bitter and alcoholic brew. Guinness is a popular and widely available stout. The English version is sometimes called "milk stout." Imperial Stout is a strong, rich, aromatic ale originally brewed for shipment from England to Tsarist Russia. Dublin Stout is even stronger. Sounds great, doesn't it. It is.

Barley Wine. Deep gold to ebony in color, with pronounced maltiness and hoppiness, barley wine exhibits a winey smoothness due to its lengthy maturation, and has the highest alcohol level of any beer. The Scottish version is known as "wee heavy."

Brown Ale. This is essentially the bottled version of a dark, mild ale. It is rich without being filling.

Wheat Beer. Usually a golden, refreshing summer drink with 35 to 50 percent wheat mixed with the barley.

LAGER

Lager differs from its cousin, ale, in several major respects. Its cultural roots are in Germany and Czechoslovakia. Lager is bottom-fermented and stored for longer periods, and tends to be lighter and more refreshing than ale. Lager generally has a less pronounced hop flavor, is less bitter, and is often less alcoholic. The following are the main lager styles.

Pilsner or Pale Lager. This is the main style of commercial beer in America. It is pale, clear, light, crisp, lightly hopped, and heavily carbonated. Examples are Budweiser, Miller, and Michelob.

Dark Lager. Similar to light lager in taste, body, and carbonation. The dark color (reddish-brown to ebony) comes from roasted grains.

Bock. Bock has more alcohol than most beers. It is deep-gold to brown-black and has a malty body, moderate hop flavor, and a sweet finish.

The Bettmann Archive

OTHER BEERS

Here are a few other beer terms you may encounter.

Abbey Beer. This is not a distinctive style, but a designation for beers brewed under licensing agreements with certain monasteries and abbeys in Belgium.

Altbier. A traditional German ale. *Alt* means "old," to distinguish the beer from the "new" lagers of the mid-19th century.

Amber Beer. A term that distinguishes beers of a medium color from "pale" and "dark" styles.

Cream Ale. An American term for a mild, pale, light-bodied ale.

Kolsch. A pale, golden, light ale.

Lambic. A unique Belgian beer, spontaneously fermented by airborne wild yeasts. Lambics are often flavored with fruits, such as cherries or raspberries. They are aged in the bottle, and can be stored anywhere from three months to four years before serving.

Light Beer. Either low-calorie or low-alcohol beer, usually made by a major brewer.

Rauchbier. Smoked beer, made with smoke-cured malt.

Steam Beer. A beer produced with a hybrid fermentation process, using bottom yeast fermented at top-yeast temperatures. It's the style of brewing used by San Francisco's Anchor Steam company.

Arcane Brews

The fascinating *Dictionary of Beer and Brewing* lists gallons of arcane beers through the ages:

Aca. Maize beer brewed in Peru since 200 B.C.

Balche. Mead made by the Maya of the Yucatan, mentioned by an explorer in 1578; it was probably a purgative.

Bi-kal. A heavy beer of ancient Sumeria.

Bilbil. A beer once brewed in Upper Egypt from durrah, a type of sorghum. The name comes from bulbul, "mother of the nightingale," because it caused drinkers to sing.

Bi-se-Bar. A light barley beer of ancient Sumeria.

Boza. A millet beer made in ancient Babylonia and Egypt (3000 to 2000 B.C.). Boza is also the term for Ethiopian wheat beer and for a nonalcoholic corn beer in Turkey.

Braga. A mild mead of medieval Russia.

Bragot. An ancient Welsh drink consisting of beer, honey, cinnamon, and galingale.

Brumalis Canna. A foamy and aromatic beer made from ginger and fruit in medieval France.

Chang. A ceremonial beer brewed from

barley in Nepal and Tibet.

Chica. The name given to *aca,* the maize beer of the Incas, by the Spanish conquistadors.

Chiu. A type of wheat beer made in China during the Han Dynasty (202 B.C.–A.D. 220), which later became the predominant beer style of China.

Chung. A Tibetan beer made from grim, a type of native barley.

Gruitbier. A European beer flavored with a mixture of herbs and spices, produced from the Middle Ages to the 15th century.

Hoan tsie'u. A type of Chinese sake.

Kaffir beer. The traditional beverage of the Bantu tribes of Africa. It was traditionally prepared from millet and was first brewed commercially in Salisbury, Rhodesia (now Zimbabwe), in 1908. Today it is typically brewed from sorghum. It is neither hopped nor filtered, contains large amounts of particulate matter, and is sold in an active state of fermentation.

Kaoliang. A sorghum beer made in China during the Sung Dynasty (960–1278).

Kava. A Polynesian beerlike beverage brewed from the roots of the kava plant.

Kvass. A Russian drink made by fermenting rye bread and flavoring it with berries. Kvass was brewed by early Slavs 2,000 years ago.

Luda. Beer of the Ossets, a Caucasian tribe of Aryan tongue and Iranian descent. They built a 600-liter beer reservoir in 600 B.C.

P'ei. A beer made in China during the Tang Dynasty (618–907), also called "floating ants" because of the refuse of grain on the surface.

Pombe. A beery drink made from millet in Guinea.

Takju. A type of Korean rice beer.

T'ien tsiou. The name given to millet beer in Chinese texts dating back to 2000 B.C.

Tiswin. An Apache Indian beer made from corn, wheat, jimson, and water (jimsonweed is poisonous).

How to
DRINK
Beer

any people believe that bottled or canned beer can never taste as good as draft beer. There is some truth to this. Packaged beer is often full of shelf-life chemicals, it's gassier, it's pasteurized, and the higher carbonation produces a bite on the tongue that can deaden the tastebuds.

There are many exquisite bottled beers (cans are another matter entirely), but if you have a choice, drink draft. In Seattle, draft beer is typically served in a pint or a schooner. A pint is the larger, straight-sided glass; a schooner is the smaller, slightly curved glass.

If you drink beer at home, where you probably don't have a dozen microbrews on tap, there are still ways to optimize the experience. Begin with proper care and handling of the brew.

First, buy fresh beer. Some conscientious breweries, such as Redhook, date their bottles. If you don't see any dates, buy beer the way you'd buy any other perishable product at the grocery store—reach toward the back of the cooler, where the latest delivery is stored. (Incidentally, because hops are harvested once a year in the fall, beer at the store or at the bar will have a fresher hop flavor in the fall and winter.)

When you get the beer home, don't let it become overheated, shaken up, or overchilled. Keep it in a cool, dark place, namely your refrigerator. The ideal storage temperature is between 40 and 50 degrees; the best spot is the warmest shelf in the fridge. Store the beer upright, not on its side. Unlike wine, which is corked, beer has a metal cap, and when the liquid comes in contact with the cap it can pick up a metallic flavor. Upright storage also minimizes oxidation between the enclosed air and the beer in the bottle. Don't store beer in the rack on the refrigerator door; the opening and closing can result in a beautiful fountain of beer when you open the bottle. The temperature fluctuations are also harmful.

And finally, don't store beer for extended periods. Most beer does not improve with age. Buy it, take it home, and drink it.

Whether you are at home or on the town, relax and enjoy your beer. Take your time. Drinking beer is fun, not a challenge. *The Guinness Book of Records* used to list a number of guzzling records. Most—including the record for "upside-down" drinking—were held by an Englishman named Peter G. Dowdeswell. A Pennsylvanian named Steve Petrosian held the American record, 1 liter in 1.3 seconds. Guinness has stopped listing these so as not to encourage health-threatening drinking practices, which is probably a good idea. While these records are weirdly compelling, they seem to miss the point.

"I drink no more than a sponge."
—Rabelais

Beer is to be savored, not chugged. Go slow.

Next, try your beer a little warmer. This notion is hard to get across to Americans, since it conjures up images of Englishmen drinking pints of hot beer. But nobody is recommending actual warm beer—just not ice-cold beer. Well-made beer is a beverage of flavor, and thicker beers, as you may have sensed intuitively, are better at warmer temperatures. This isn't too important with ordinary thirst-quenching American beer, but a complex ale will taste best at about 50° F, a quality stout or porter at even a few degrees warmer than that. So pull the beer out of the refrigerator and let it sit at room temperature for 10 minutes before pouring it. When you're served an ale in a tavern, let it rest for a few minutes before you sip.

There are a number of major disadvantages to serving beer too cold. As with all foods, the flavors are inhibited at lower temperatures because the aromatics are not released as quickly. The low temperature also numbs the tastebuds a little. And finally, cold beer tends to be gassier, which means that you'll be gassier, too.

Don't drink straight out of the bottle, because that's also gassier. When you pour the beer into a glass, some of the carbon dioxide is released. Of course, you can drink beer out of a ceramic stein or a paper cup or a coffee mug, but clean glass has aesthetic advantages. For one thing, you can enjoy the color of the beer, and the visual aspect adds to the drinking experience. Howard Hillman, in his *Gourmet Guide to Beer*, even advocates drinking beer

"Beer, happy Produce of our Isle / Can sinewy Strength Impart, / And wearied with Fatigue and Toil / Can cheer each manly Heart.

Continued on next page

out of a brandy snifter, because the tulip shape captures and focuses the aromas.

Pour the beer gently right down the middle of the glass, not down the side. Pouring it down the middle produces a full head, and that enhances the beer's bouquet. The down-the-side approach probably became popular for a couple of reasons: people saw bartenders do it to draw off foam when kegs were gassy or newly tapped, and they saw it done on TV commercials, in which down-the-side looks more elegant than the plop-plop of down-the-middle. A perhaps-unnecessary word of caution: pouring beer quickly can be exciting, but it is often followed by a familiar exercise involving a bar towel. So anytime you see too much of a head forming, switch to down-the-side.

Quality beers have thick, dense heads—as tall as an inch or more. In Seattle, though, head

"Genius of Health, thy grateful Taste / Rivals the Cup of Jove, / And warms each English generous Breast / With Liberty and Love."
—**Caption for the William Hogarth engraving called** *Beer Street* **(1751)**

expectations have to be adjusted because beer at sea level will have considerably less head than at high

elevations. A beer should hold its head for a while. (Not everybody agrees about the charms of a full head. Some drinkers think foam merely robs them of their full glass of beer.)

Enjoy the beer's appearance. Hold the glass up to the light. Savor the color. Beer hues range from golden to ruby to ebony. The bubbles should be small, and should rise to the top at a slow, relaxed speed, the pace you should emulate in drinking the brew. Incidentally, if bubbles cling to the side of the glass, the glass isn't perfectly clean.

After you've poured, inhale. Actually, take a pretty good sniff. The genteel whiff appropriate when evaluating wine doesn't work with beer because the distinguishing odorants in beer are less intense than those in a typical wine. You'll smell malt, hops, and yeast. The pleasing bitterness of hops balanced with the natural sweetness of barley malt is a tonic that increases the appetite for both brew and food. Your beer should smell clean and fresh.

And finally, to get the most out of any good beer, drink it very slowly, but don't sip it. Beers are really for gulping, because the tastebuds that respond to bitterness are on the back of the tongue. Swish it and swirl it around in your mouth for a few seconds. As beer writer Will Anderson says, try actually chewing it. Is the beer thick or thin? Is it all bubbles, or does the carbonation feel good against your tongue and mouth? Swallow and consider the aftertaste. It should be pleasant and leave your mouth feeling good.

Too Much of a Good Thing

Drinking any amount of alcohol can impair your ability to drive. The alcohol concentration in your body depends on your weight, the amount of food in your stomach (a full stomach will postpone alcohol absorption but will not keep you from becoming drunk), the period of time during which you consume alcohol, and the period of time since your last drink. Generally speaking, anything more than a couple of beers in an hour will impair your driving.

If you are under 150 pounds, you'll have impaired driving ability after consuming two drinks (12-ounce beers) in an hour. If you drink four beers in three hours, you'll probably be legally drunk, and you definitely shouldn't drive. If you weigh 180 pounds or more, your driving will be impaired after three drinks in an hour, or four to five beers in a three-hour period.

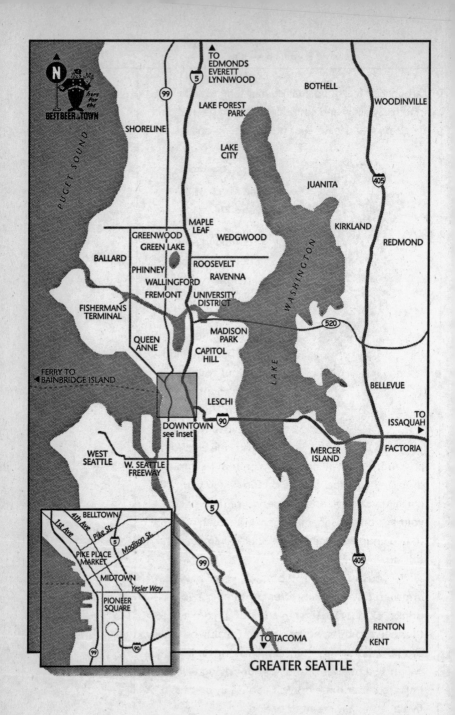

GREATER SEATTLE

The Insider's Guide to Neighborhood
BREWPUBS
and Microbreweries

Greater Seattle

All taverns may not be as imaginatively named as Humpty's Dump, just off the highway near Eugene, or Thirsty's in Seattle (which gave way to the equally imaginative name Re-bar). But good names are part of the fun of American bar culture. Here are a few from Seattle: Alias Mac's, Bigfoot Inn, The Blinker, The Borderline,

Continued on next page

There are beerific places to drink in neighborhoods all over Seattle. They come in many sizes, styles, and price ranges. Their attractions are many and varied. One place may be notable for fabulous food, another for wild decor, a third for its panoramic view, and a fourth for its distinctive customers. But, of course, the enjoyment of beer has a great deal to do with the moment, the mood, the weather, the ambience, whom you're with, or what you've just eaten. The overriding guiding criterion for this book was to seek out the places that are simply comfortable and friendly.

Many modern eating and drinking establishments have nonsmoking sections and some are entirely nonsmoking. The symbol ⊘ indicates a nonsmoking establishment.

PIONEER SQUARE

The Pacific Northwest Brewing Company
322 Occidental Ave S
621-7002
Mon-Thurs 4 PM-midnight, Fri & Sat 4 PM-1 AM,
Sun noon-8 PM

This spacious brewpub, which produced its first beer in May 1989, is located in the pedestrian promenade in Pioneer Square, right next to the popular Torrefazione coffee roaster and several art galleries. Customers can watch the brewers at work, and the spacious brewpub's gleaming tanks, warm wood, red brick interior, and large windows make a pleasant setting. In warm weather an outdoor patio is open, providing a European atmosphere. Because it's near the Kingdome, Pacific Northwest is also a popular pre-game spot. The menu includes sausages, soups, seafood, and sandwiches. The beers are in a bitter, English style: Blond, Bitter, Gold, Amber, Stout, and Winter Brau.

Bubba's, The Crazy Norwegian, The Fire-Dog, The Flip Side, The Ginza, Goofy's, The Laundromat, Lucky 7, Marco Polo, The Midget, Mike's Chili Parlor, The Monkey, Moonraker, The Pick & Shovel, R-Low's, The Rollin Log, The Ron Dee Voo, The Rose Garden, The Siren, Snappy, Tak & Toni's Dome Stadium, Uncle Mo's Watering Hole, The Yardarm.

MIDTOWN

Noggins Brewery
400 Pine St (in Westlake Center)
682-2739
Mon-Thurs 9 AM-11 PM, Fri & Sat 9 AM-midnight,
Sun 9 AM-9 PM

CLOSED

This brewpub is on an upper floor of the popular Westlake Center retail complex in the heart of the downtown shopping district. In addition to a bar, it has a couple of dining areas that look out through vast windows at the ornate brickwork and activity of Westlake Plaza below. Noggins serves a fairly complete food menu (it's in an area of Westlake Center devoted to various fast food outlets). It also has occasional jazz groups or comedy acts. There are usually five or six beers on tap, which might include Special Old Bitter, Noggins Pale Ale, India Pale Ale, Dark Ale, Scottish Ale, Autumn Alt, Barleywine, Weizen Brau, Dunkel Weizen, Hefeweizen, porter, stout, and lagers.

PIKE PLACE MARKET

Pike Place Brewery

1432 Western Ave
622-3373; 622-1880
Tues-Sat 10 AM-5 PM,
Sun & Mon noon-4 PM

Pike Place Brewery is not a brewpub, although the beers can be purchased at the brewery. It was founded in 1989 and is one of Seattle's smaller microbreweries. Owner Charles Finkel has a long history in the food marketing and importing business, particularly with wine. Finkel also runs Liberty Malt Supply, the homebrewing supply shop next door, and Merchant du Vin, one of America's premier beer importing businesses.

Pike Place Brewery's beers include Pike Place Pale Ale; East Indian Pale Yellow; XXXXX Stout ("Five-X"); the potent Old Bawdy barley wine; seasonal beers such as Cervesa Rosanna, flavored with hot peppers; and an ale spiced with oregano. The beers are available in kegs at the brewery, and sometimes in bottles at the brewery or grocery stores, although Finkel says that "the demand exceeds the supply."

At his offices, Charles Finkel took a break from designing a new beer label on his Macintosh computer and talked about beer.

Q: Why did you want to operate a brewery yourself?

Finkel: My friends are brewers. So I have to be a brewer to be the equal of my peers.

Q: Do you go along with the idea that Seattle's weather is moody like England's, and consequently we want to sit around the fire and drink a hearty ale?

Finkel [laughing]: Do you sit around the fire and drink a lot of hearty ale? I'd like to do that. I think people choose to live in Seattle or Portland because they're civilized places in the world that would suggest a lifestyle that would include wholesome, healthy, temperate beverages. And beer falls into those categories.

Q: Do you think the American consumer just jumps on exotic beers as a trend, or is there genuine interest?

Finkel: In America, we are a dichotomy. In one way we aspire to great tradition, but on the other hand, we are very trendy. Those two can coexist when there are a lot of good trends—which there are in this subject. You can't go wrong.

"There is nothing which has yet been contrived by man by which so much happiness is produced as by a good tavern or inn."
—Samuel Johnson

FREMONT

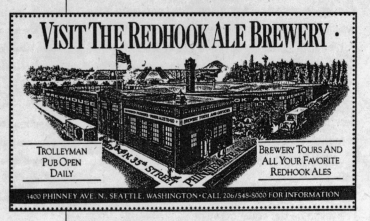

· VISIT THE REDHOOK ALE BREWERY ·

TROLLEYMAN
PUB OPEN
DAILY

BREWERY TOURS AND
ALL YOUR FAVORITE
REDHOOK ALES

3400 PHINNEY AVE. N., SEATTLE, WASHINGTON·CALL 206/548-8000 FOR INFORMATION

Redhook Ale Brewery / The Trolleyman
3400 Phinney Ave N
548-8000
Mon-Fri 8:30 AM-11 PM, Sat 11 AM-11 PM, Sun noon-6 PM

The Trolleyman is the pub for Redhook Ale
Brewery, the largest of the independent Seattle
breweries. The pub is in the same fabulously restored
brick and green-trimmed building as the brewery
itself, the historic Fremont Trolley Car Barn just north
of the Ship Canal. The Trolleyman is light and airy,
with a wooden ceiling and white walls, artwork, a red-
and-gray floor, and plants in terra-cotta pots. There's
a long, curved bar, white tables with high-backed
wooden chairs, and comfortable overstuffed chairs in
a fireplace area. An excellent snack menu is
announced on an easel board: lasagne, steak and
mushroom pie, black bean soup. The taped music
ranges from classical to R&B, and there are occasional
live performances. Also available are souvenirs such as
shirts and glassware, plus tours of the brewery.

Redhook Ale Brewery was founded in 1981 by Paul Shipman and Gordon Bowker (also a founder of Seattle's Starbucks Coffee). They astutely recognized that there was nationwide growth in the import beer market, and that the per capita consumption of draft beer in the Seattle area was the highest in the country. Redhook began making beer in Ballard, which had both light industrial facilities and a strong European tradition. On August 11, 1982, the brewery sold its first pint of Redhook Ale, a rich ale with an herbal character that favors sweetness over bitterness. Redhook produced 1,000 barrels the first year. The brewery introduced Blackhook Porter, a well-hopped London-style porter, in June 1983, and Ballard Bitter, a classic pub-style English bitter, in the spring of 1984. They later began making Redhook ESB (Extra Special Bitter). Redhook began bottling its beer in 1985, and eventually outgrew its original quarters.

Brewing at the new location in Fremont began in September 1988. An expansion in 1991 gave Redhook a brewing capacity of 60,000 barrels a year, about the size of Anchor Steam. About 60 percent of the brewery's sales are in ESB, some 30 percent in Ballard Bitter, and about 10 percent in Blackhook Porter. Two-thirds of the sales are in the Puget Sound area, although Redhook does business down the West Coast as far as Palo Alto.

After a short tour of the brewery, which was just completing its expansion, Redhook president Paul Shipman sat in front of the fireplace in the Trolleyman for an interview.

Q: Redhook is quite a bit bigger than the other local microbrewers, isn't it?

The world record for beer-keg lifting belongs to Irishman Tommy Gaskin, who raised a keg of beer weighing 137.79 pounds over his head 656 times in six hours at Newry, Northern Ireland, on October 28, 1989.

"Beer has long been the prime lubricant in our social intercourse and the sacred throat-anointing fluid that accompanies the ritual of mateship. To sink a few cold ones with the blokes is both an escape and a confirmation of belonging."
—Rennie Ellis, on beer drinking in Australia, in *The New York Times*, March 13, 1985

Shipman: That's right. You have the Big Three—Budweiser, Miller, and Coors. Then you have what I call the Little Three—Anchor Steam, Sierra Nevada, and Redhook. We're the littlest of the Little Three. We're the newest. The other two are in the California market, which is a huge market.

Q: As you look at it today, what turned you into a beer drinker and put you into the business?

Shipman: I was exposed to a lot of European beers. I'm acclimated to a wide range of tastes. The national beer in the United States is very reasonably priced. It's fresh, for the most part, but it is very narrow in terms of its taste profile. They just don't go for the flavor experimentation. They satisfy the largest possible audience. We're not into that at all.

Q: Why do you think the Northwest has this thing for microbrews?

Shipman: The people who live in this part of the country are not only more experimental, but they are more likely to reject the idea of a national beer. They desire something that belongs to them. They're independent in terms of their thought. The climate supports the idea of fuller, richer flavor. In California, specialty beers, microbrewery beers, are still kind of a novelty. In the Northwest, they're part of life. People no longer view them as an alternative; they're central to the way people drink beer.

Q: Do you like the idea of all these little one-man breweries popping up?

Shipman: I think it's fabulous, I think it's great. We started out like that. I enjoy drinking the variety of beers that's available in the Northwest.

Q: Every place around here has Redhook, right?

Shipman: Pretty much. There are 600

neighborhood taverns and pubs in Seattle, and we're probably in about 400 to 500 of them. I like them all. I like the variety of pubs as much as I like the variety of beers.

UNIVERSITY DISTRICT

Big Time Brewery and Alehouse
4133 University Way NE
545-4509
Daily 11:30 AM-12:30 AM

Located on University Way amid the usual collegiate trappings—coffeehouses, ethnic restaurants, quick-copy shops, and T-shirt stores—this wholesome brewpub serves three or four American ales, all brewed on the premises and on tap. As at most brewpubs, you can view the brewing process from inside the pub—not that there's a lot to see other than the brewkettles which produce 14-barrel batches, and the other equipment. The beer is sold in kegs, or you can bring in a container and have it filled.

The 135-seat Big Time, which opened in 1988, is a blend of timeless student tavern and quintessentially modern brewpub: vintage breweriana, lots of wood, and an 80-year-old bar. Signs advertise such arcane suds as Beuwyck Beer-Ales, Van Dyke Lager Beer, Western Brew Beer, and "Switch to Topper Pilsener." A stuffed dinosaur head looms over the bar, and music booms from the jukebox.

The crowd is always lively—studentish, but not sub-adult—and the sandwiches, soups, and nachos seem to march nonstop from the little kitchen. A back room has a TV and a shuffleboard table. Big Time, bless it, also has a nonsmoking section right next to the big windows that look into the brewery itself. Always on tap are Prime Time Pale Ale, Atlas Amber Ale, and Coal Creek Porter. Specialty beers include Watertown Wheat, All Out Stout, Slam Dunkel Weizen Bock, Bhagwan's Best India Pale Ale, Old Wooly Barleywine Ale, and Julefest, a Christmas ale.

BALLARD

Maritime Pacific Brewery
1514 NW Leary Way
782-6181
Mon-Fri 6 AM-6 PM, Sat 11-6 PM
Tours Sat 11-6—on weekdays, by appointment only

George Hancock's Maritime Pacific Brewery opened in 1990 in a brick building at the Ballard end of the Ballard Bridge. There's no brewpub attached, but you can buy the beer there, and a tasting room is planned. Maritime is a visible storefront, but hardly in a conventional retail neighborhood: it's across the street from Ballard Auto Wrecking and tucked in between Miller Paint and Scott Galvanizing Company. The Maritime space used to be a transmission shop.

Hancock produces three beers year-round, and adds four seasonal brews at different times during the year. Flagship Red Ale, the brewery's mainstay, is an altbier with 20 percent wheat; Navigator Dark is a heavy, dark holiday ale; Nightwatch, which Hancock describes as "a true Northwest hybrid," is a cross between a Bavarian lager and a porter; Clipper Gold is a refreshing wheaten; and Bosun's Black Ale is a dark porter.

Hancock sat in the office of his spotless brewery fielding questions about his business, answering the phone, and getting up to wheel kegs out to distributors' trucks at his garage doors.

Q: Why did you get into the brewing business?

Hancock: I was a homebrewer back in the early '70s, and my life has always been around beer. I've traveled a lot through England and Germany, and I enjoy the different aspects of the ales. The beer industry is an extension of cooking, creating a recipe. So I look at it like an extension of the restaurant that I always wanted to have, but I'm not a restauranteur.

Out of college, I didn't work with my fine arts degree. I worked in a geotechnical instrumentation company. I hate to say it, but making belt buckles and things like that, I really wasn't going to make a lot of money. And to be honest with you, I knew I was too staid. When I finally said, "It's time for a career change, I'm going to do what I want to do now," this was what I wanted to do.

Q: Do you think there is a Northwest style of ale?

Hancock: I feel there is no set recipe. We can do whatever we want to do. We're a conglomerate of

"When I was a young girl / I used to seek pleasure / When I was a young girl / I used to drink ale / Right out of the alehouse / And into the jailhouse"
—"When I Was a Young Girl," English drinking song

Water is a better thirst-quencher than beer. The body absorbs water more quickly because it has fewer suspended solids.

different flavors, different tastes, different attitudes. That's what makes the Northwest so unique. That's what makes all the beers so distinctive in this area. If we were a homogeneous group, we'd all be drinking Budweiser, or Rainier, or something like that.

Q: Do you think that Seattle consumers are more adventuresome?

Hancock: I think they're adventuresome. One, you have the diehard Seattleites. Then you have the new people, the influx—they've come here, this is Nirvana. So when they come here they'll have more of an open mind. They're always searching for new flavors. Which is frustrating for us brewers, because we're always trying to get a little bit of the public to try our ales and stay with them.

Q: Do you like the notion of the beer gourmet?

Hancock: Microbrews have got more complexity, more depth, than your normal domestics. The only thing that I don't want to see happen is quote-unquote beer snobbery. It takes the socialness out of drinking beer. Appreciate it as a beer. Don't drink it as something you have to break down and analyze.

WEST SEATTLE

California and Alaska Street Brewing Company
4720 California Ave SW
938-2476
Tues-Thurs 2-11 PM,
Fri & Sat 2 PM-midnight,
Sun 4-9 PM

The California and Alaska opened in late 1991 just south of the Junction, the main intersection of West Seattle's shopping district. It's across the street from several ethnic restaurants and near Meredith's 10-Cent Store, Poggie Tavern, and Dogmeat's Harley-Davidson Accessories. Possibly the best thing about the California and Alaska is its most unusual aspect, one that reflects the changing expectations of the American beer drinker: the place is entirely non-smoking.

The low-ceilinged, wood-paneled front section is filled with tables and opens up into a two-story area at the back that holds the bar and all the brewing equipment. The place was sparely decorated just a few months after opening but it will likely acquire more character and decor as time goes on. It's not too loud; it's a place to talk. The pub serves a small menu of sandwiches and soups and four or five beers, ranging from a heavy porter to a light, wheaten-style ale.

KIRKLAND

Hale's Ales Ltd.
109 Central Way
827-4359
Mon-Fri 8 AM-5 PM

Hale's is a microbrewery, not a brewpub, but it is right next to the Kirkland Roaster restaurant, which has big windows in the bar that look right into Mike Hale's operation, much in the manner of a

The Latin word *bibere* means "to drink," and the Saxon word *baere* means barley. The term "beer" did not come into common use until the Celtic word *beor* was applied to the malt brew produced in the monasteries of northern Gaul.

brewpub. Hale's Ales started in Colville, in eastern Washington, and became so popular that the Kirkland brewery was opened in 1987. Hale's is in the quaint old Moss Bay section of downtown Kirkland, near the waterfront.

Hale's Ales, which are pretty widely available at drinkeries around town, include Hale's Pale American Ale, the brewery's original brew and number-one seller; the emphatically hopped Special Bitter, basically a super-unleaded version of the American Ale; mahogany-brown Celebration Porter; Washington Wheat, a golden ale; Wee Heavy, a potent winter brew in the style of a barley wine—strong and malty ("wee heavy" is the traditional Scottish term for a strong ale); Irish Ale, a "session beer," meaning that it is satisfying but low in alcohol, and so it can be consumed steadily all evening; O'Brien Harvest Ale, made with the fresh hops of the annual fall harvest; and Cascade Mist, a lager-like summer ale.

Hale's also has a Moss Bay line: Moss Bay Amber, the type of ale that in England might be referred to as an "ordinary bitter" (but can you imagine Americans—even beer gourmets—ordering a beer with such a lackluster name as "ordinary bitter"?); Moss Bay Extra, basically the amber made bigger in every way—a classic Northwest Bitter and a huge mouthful of malt and hops; and the black and strong Moss Bay Stout, which Hale's calls "the espresso of our ales."

During a visit to Hale's Kirkland brewery, a small storefront-sized operation, founder Mike Hale talked about his operation.

Q: Is Hale's considered real small or more in the middle, as microbreweries go?

Hale: We're kind of in the middle. We started off a year behind Grant's and Redhook, in '83. We've been kind of keeping pace with Grant's. Redhook has really taken off. We're at about 8,000 barrels a year.

Q: When you first got into brewing, did you foresee that it would be a big, booming fad and a business?

Hale: I had no idea. I was just having some fun. I'm kind of a mechanical sort of guy, so I built the brewery myself. And then I was just fascinated with the process. It's all natural—nature does the majority of the work. We herd the stuff together and it makes itself. We just provide the environment and the opportunity.

Q: What was your first account?

Hale [laughing]: It takes a unique individual, first of all. The first account was in Colville—it was the Viking Tavern. It went off with a bang. Everybody had heard about it, everybody was interested in it. And the guy was doing a keg-a-day, seven-kegs-a-week account. Even today, that's a killer account. So that was about my capacity. Working by myself, one brew a week, about 20 kegs a week. Our first account in Spokane was Clinkerdagger's restaurant, and they're still pouring the beer. And our first account in Seattle was the Deluxe II.

Q: How many places in Seattle have Hale's now?

Hale: A hundred, 120 or so. That's what I like about staying small. I still get involved in making the beer, although I get a little bit more removed. But every once in a while I get to actually make some. I get to deliver it sometimes.

Q: You sell to bars and taverns but you don't bottle your beer. Why is that?

Hale: Just the process of bottling oxygenates the beer and gets a jump on aging. Bottled beer's a compromise, so why compromise? We're already in the business of not compromising. And we're selling all we can make anyway, so what difference does it make?

Q: Do you distribute in Oregon or anywhere?

Hale: We don't go very far because we don't make that much, for one thing. And the concern for freshness. We've had people ask for our beer from California. They've said, "Well, we'll come get it." We just said, "Well, you know, why don't you not do that. Let's don't get into that." It seems kind of trendy.

Other Washington State Breweries and Brewpubs

The Northwest microbrew revolution hasn't been confined to Seattle. Some brewers prefer more

The ancient Egyptians made beer called *hek* by crumbling barley bread into jars, filling the jars with water, and allowing the mixture to ferment. When they had to cross the desert, they carried only fermented bread crumbs. When they reached an oasis they added water, and voilá—instant beer.

bucolic settings. So, from Poulsbo to Yakima, craft brewers are perfecting the brewmaker's art.

KALAMA

Hart Brewing
110 Marine Dr
673-2962
Tours: Mon-Fri
8 AM-5 PM

Hart Brewing, makers of the renowned Pyramid Ales, is located a few hours south of Seattle in the shadow of Mount St. Helens. It was founded in 1984, and a few years ago, it moved from a turn-of-the-century general store into a spacious new facility that is an attractive showcase for the beer. Hart offers tours and sells labels, coasters, T-shirts, and lapel pins. The ales, which are fairly widely distributed in Seattle pubs, taverns, and grocery stores, include the malty and highly hopped Pyramid Pale Ale; the lighter and refreshing Pyramid Wheaten Ale; the milder Pacific Crest Ale; the dark and hearty Sphinx Stout; and Snow Cap Ale, a barley winelike, heavily hopped winter ale.

George Washington maintained a small brewery at Mount Vernon. He favored porter.

POULSBO

Thomas Kemper Brewing Company
The Tap Room

22381 Foss Rd NE
697-1446 (Seattle number: 682-2634)
Sun-Thurs 11 AM-6 PM, Fri & Sat 11 AM-7 PM

Founded in 1984, Thomas Kemper Brewing operates the Tap Room as its brewpub. The brewery is located in the woods a few miles outside of Poulsbo on the Kitsap Peninsula. To get there from Seattle, take the Winslow ferry; the brewery is just a short drive north of Winslow. The whole trip takes about an hour and a half. The rustic brewpub serves lunches and has a beer garden. It's a restful place, surrounded by quiet farmland and forest. An Oktoberfest Celebration is held on the grounds the third weekend in September.

Unlike most Northwest breweries, which make ale, Kemper makes bottom-fermenting Bavarian-style lagers. They are aged at 33° F for a month after brewing. The beers include the European pilsner-style Helles Lager, a darker Dunkel Lager, Rolling Bay Bock, plus a pilsner and seasonal brews. Thomas Kemper also makes a couple of nonalcoholic products, a tangy birch beer, and a rich root beer that has become popular in Seattle. The brewery offers tours and sells T-shirts, mugs, sweatshirts, polo shirts, hats, and aprons.

ROSLYN

Roslyn Brewing Company

33 Pennsylvania Ave
(509) 649-2232
Sat & Sun 12-5 PM

Roslyn is an hour and a half east of Seattle on I-90, over Snoqualmie Pass, not too far from the ski areas. The town itself garnered fame in the early '90s as the location for the TV show "Northern Exposure." Around the turn of the century, Roslyn was a coal-mining town and featured 24 saloons, many of which served beer made by the Roslyn Brewing and Malting Company (it was closed by Prohibition in 1913). The new Roslyn microbrewery was built on the town's main street by Dino Enrico, whose great-grandparents were among Roslyn's immigrant pioneers. The beer is available at the brewery and a few other outlets. There is a nice little bar with a few tables at the brewery, where a customer can sit and drink. But they're only open for a few hours on weekends, so call to make sure they're open.

YAKIMA

Yakima Brewing & Malting Company
The Brewery Pub

32 N Front St
(509) 575-2922
Mon-Sat 11:30 AM-11 PM, Sun 11:30 AM-8:30 PM

Many beer historians consider the Grant's Ales

brewpub to be the granddaddy of the American brewpub movement. Yakima Brewing & Malting was started in 1982 by Bert Grant, who is in turn considered a godfather of the American microbrewing movement. The brewery is in the Yakima Valley, one of the world's leading hop-growing regions. Grant's beers are famous for being fiercely hopped. They include the deep red Scottish Ale; a refreshing India Pale Ale; the rich, sweet, black, potent Imperial Stout; and the milder Celtic Ale. Grant's also makes a golden Weis Bier and a Hard Cider. All are widely available in Seattle bars and supermarkets.

In late 1991, Yakima Brewing & Malting moved into a new two-million-dollar, 25,000-barrel-a-year, state-of-the-art facility. The original brewpub was a crowded, 35-seat room next door to the brewery. The new 250-seat, oak-and-brick brewpub has a fireplace, a glassed-in sunroom, dartboards, railroad memorabilia, a beer glass and bottle collection, a sword collection, and stained-glass windows. There's occasionally live jazz music. The brewpub offers sandwiches, soups, salads, and desserts, and also more ambitious ethnic-cuisine specials. You can also order coffee, tea, or lemonade. The place is entirely nonsmoking.

The Insider's Guide to Greater Seattle's Neighborhood
ALEHOUSES
and Bars

COLLEGE INN
PUB

PIONEER SQUARE

**"I would give all
my fame for a
pot of ale, and
safety."
—Shakespeare,
*Henry V***

Doc Maynard's

600 First Ave
682-4649
Sun-Thurs 9 AM-4 PM, Fri & Sat 8 PM-2 AM

Doc Maynard's is in the heart of Pioneer Square,
on the little triangle that contains the pergola and the
totem pole. It's a restaurant, a nightclub, and the
headquarters for the Seattle Underground Tour,
which takes tourists to the below-street-level remains
of the business district that burned down in the Great
Seattle Fire of 1889. During the day, Doc Maynard's
serves business people and tourists. At night, it's a
lively rock-and-roll club.

F.X. McRory's

419 Occidental Ave S
623-4800
Mon-Fri 11:30 AM-2 AM, Sat & Sun 3 PM-2 AM

F.X. McRory's, a sports
bar and restaurant, has a
vast beer department with
26 shiny taps pouring most
of the Northwest's
microbrews—Moss Bay,
Grant's, Pyramid, Ballard
Bitter, Widmer, Full Sail, and others—
as well as Anchor, Harp, and Samuel Adams. McRory's
owner Mick McHugh organized the area's first
Microbrew Festival in August 1984, and has been one
of the city's leading proponents of local breweries and

their rich, flavorful ales, lagers, and stouts. During its annual Great Northwest Beer Festival, McRory's dedicates 24 taps to Northwest microbrews for a full month, and the bar serves up a festival sampler package: three six-ounce tastings. During the holiday season, the bar dedicates a dozen taps to Christmas beers and ales.

The main room is a quintessential sports bar, hung with team pennants and LeRoy Neiman oil paintings of vaguely familiar sports events. Huge TV sets loom in every corner (although, in fairness, they aren't on all the time). A board touting "The World's Largest Collection of Bourbon" lists about 90 different brands. Custom coffee is always brewing, and McRory's also has an acclaimed oyster bar and an extensive dining menu. F.X. McRory's is a huge full-service saloon right next to the Kingdome, so naturally it's a popular watering hole for the sporting crowd as well as local and visiting pro athletes. On a quiet afternoon, it's warm and pleasant. On a busy night, it's a rugby scrum.

The J&M Cafe

201 First Ave S
624-1670
Daily 10:30 AM-2 AM

The J&M is a beautiful example of a Pioneer Square saloon. It's one of Seattle's oldest bars, and it has antique stained-glass windows to prove it. They sit up high and announce "J&M Cafe and Cardroom." The place doesn't have a large beer selection, but it's a decent place to quaff a Blackhook Porter. It also has a satisfying sandwich and soup menu. The bar is

The strongest beer in the world is the aptly named Roger & Out, brewed at the Frog & Parrot in Sheffield, England. It has an alcohol content of 16.9 percent. First brewed in 1985, Roger & Out took the title away from longtime record-holder Samichlaus Bier from Brauerei Hürlimann of Zurich, Switzerland, which is 13.94 percent alcohol. Another strong one is Kulminator, with 13.2 percent alcohol, a double bock brewed in Kulmbach, Germany.

"The troubles of
our proud and
angry dust / Are
from eternity,
and shall not
fall. / Bear them
we can, and if we
must / Shoulder
the sky, my lad,
and drink your
ale."
—A. E. Housman

popular with the frat-and-bridge crowd, so on many nights it's difficult to get into the place. If you do get in, you'll find a high-volume, active scene. There's a long lunch counter/bar, as well as a regular liquor bar—a massive, mirrored creation. Ornate orange-and-black chandeliers hang from the high, white tin ceiling, and a few photos of pioneering Seattleites embellish the walls.

Merchants Cafe
109 Yesler Way
624-1515
Daily 10 AM-2 AM

The Merchants may be more interesting for what it *was* than what it is, but it's still a fine place. It's the oldest restaurant in Seattle, having opened as a saloon in 1890. As the Merchants Cafe motto says, "Don't Settle for Imitation History." The building was erected after the Great Seattle Fire in 1889 burned the downtown to the ground. The original saloon was called the Merchants Exchange Saloon. Hooks in the alley were used to lower kegs into the basement beer wells, and the huge safe was used to hold miners' assets. Today, the Merchants is a classic Pioneer Square restaurant. Upstairs, there are 10 marble-topped tables, six booths, and a 30-foot bar that came around the Horn in the late 1800s. Downstairs is a nonsmoking room with a similar number of tables.

New Orleans Cafe

114 First Ave S
622-2563
Mon-Thurs 11 AM-10 PM, Fri & Sat 11 AM-2 AM

This little restaurant and jazz club is decorated in classic Pioneer Square cum New Orleans style: brick walls hung with posters and paintings of musicians. The New Orleans is a long, narrow room with a bandstand halfway down; all the seats are pretty close, but most of them are sideways to the band. The entertainment runs from local zydeco bands and jazz groups to the occasional name act, including periodic visits from such superstars as trumpeter Dizzy Gillespie, who seems to enjoy the informal, elbow-rubbing nature of the place.

Pioneer Square Saloon

73 Yesler Way
628-6444
Daily noon-2 AM

It was music to my ears: "Do you have a light beer on tap?" asked a customer. "No, I don't," came the bartender's unapologetic reply. The beer list at the Pioneer Square Saloon isn't extensive—about 10 brews—but it's always carefully selected. It might include Navigator, Hefeweizen, or Moss Bay. There's also a decent selection of wine, nonalcoholic drinks, and food. The saloon is long and narrow with a black-and-white floor, white-topped tables, slowly turning ceiling fans, and heavy chandeliers. Paintings and other artwork hold up the walls. Standing atop the bar is a three-foot-high inflatable sculptured rendition of Edvard Munch's *The Scream*.

The ambience runs a bit to the bohemian. You see guys with long ponytails and women with jeans ripped out at the knee. People at several tables are diligently writing in notebooks. A whole adjacent section—the storefront next door, with doors cut through the wall for access—is a series of three rooms with tables, more artwork, lava lamps, darts, and a pool table. There are occasional music events, poetry readings, and other low-key happenings. In short, the place is very comfortable.

MIDTOWN

The Bookstore, A Bar
1007 First Ave (in the Alexis Hotel)
624-4844
Mon-Sat 7 AM-2 AM, Sun 2 PM-midnight

The Bookstore is an intimate literary-theme bar that offers terrific snacks from the menu of The Painted Table next door (served until 10 PM). It has the feel of a slightly high-tech library in a mansion. Frankly, a martini or a cognac goes better with The Bookstore, but the place also serves microbrews, and it's a nice, sedate place for a drink.

The Brooklyn Seafood, Steak & Oyster House
1212 Second Ave
224-7000
Mon-Thurs 11 AM-11 PM, Fri & Sat 11 AM-12:30 AM

The Brooklyn draws a crowd of business

fast-trackers who are looking either to make a few connections or to relax a little after a hard day. The trench-coat quotient is one of the highest in the city. The area just inside the front door is the bar, surrounded by barstools and tables on a raised level. On Friday afternoons, the after-work clientele overfills the room in a comfortably busy way. Everybody's in a good mood, and it's strictly standing room only. Making your way through the crowd is an exercise in "pardon me."

There are comfortable booths along the walls, half-globe chandeliers, and white-glass sconces on the walls. The dining area beyond the bar is a white-tablecloth sort of place, much quieter than the ultrasocial bar. Dinner customers sit in big booths, at tables, or at high-backed stools along a counter, where they can watch the cooks work. Although the Brooklyn serves a full menu and has a full bar, it also goes out of its way to provide beer guidance. The menu marks particular beers that go best with certain foods. A specialty is the Beer Sampler, which consists of 3.5-ounce glasses (a swallow or so) of several microbrews on tap. The Brooklyn holds a Northwest Oyster and Microbrewery Festival in the fall.

The Cloud Room (in the Camlin Hotel)

1619 Ninth Ave
682-0100
Daily 5:30 PM-2 AM

On those nights that are meant for a lounge crawl, you shouldn't miss the aerie at the top of the Camlin Hotel. You ride up the elevator (it has a special Cloud Room button) to the cozy room at the summit.

The world's largest beer bottle was 6'11" tall and 5'5¹/₂" in circumference and was displayed at the Laidley Tourist Festival in Laidley, Australia, on September 2, 1989. It was filled with 92 gallons of Laidley Gold, a wheat beer available only in Laidley.

The Cloud Room has a comfortable bar as well as table and booth seating. There is always action at the piano bar, including sing-alongs that get more vigorous as the night wears on. You can eat, and there's full bar service. The Cloud Room is close to the Paramount Theatre, so on concert nights it is packed both before and after the show. Sometimes there's even celebrity spotting, when the performers unwind at the lounge after earning their day's wages.

The Fireside Room (in the Sorrento Hotel)
900 E Madison St
622-6400
Daily 5 PM-2 AM

The ultimate in hotel lounges, the Fireside is on the main floor of the Sorrento Hotel, which is just east of downtown. The small, 76-room hotel is a beautifully restored example of pseudo-Renaissance architecture (it was modeled on a Sorrento castle). When it opened in 1909, it was the city's most elegant hotel. It eventually fell apart, but was refurbished in 1981. What was once a huge lobby is now the mahogany-lined Fireside Room. The lounge is all burnished wood, plush carpeting, and linen napkins. The Fireside Room is as comfortable as its name suggests, with plenty of sofas to sink into. The clientele is typically well-heeled hotel guests (the penthouse suite goes for $700 a night) and local drop-ins. They are often entertained by a pianist playing classical or light jazz.

Fullers (in the Sheraton Hotel)

1400 Sixth Ave
621-9000
Mon-Fri 11:30 AM-2 PM and 5:30 PM-10 PM,
Sat 5:30 PM-10 PM

Fullers has long enjoyed a national reputation as Seattle's finest restaurant, with four-star ratings in all the right places. For several years, the kitchen was run by renowned chef Caprial Pence. In 1992, Monique Barbeau took over. The food is contemporary and representative of the region. In addition to a full bar and an extensive wine list, Fullers carries a full complement of microbrews. The entire restaurant, which seats 90, is nonsmoking. The customers include hotel guests, but Fullers is also a destination dining spot for locals. The setting is quiet and formal, with light-wood-lined walls, muted lighting, and posh red armchairs at the tables. The decor features Northwest artwork, including paintings by Mark Tobey and glass from the Pilchuck School.

Jazz Alley

2033 Sixth Ave
441-9729
Mon-Sat 6:30 PM-12:30 AM

John Dimitriou's Jazz Alley is a top jazz supper club with good Northwest and Mediterranean food and internationally renowned acts featured in week-long engagements. There really isn't a bad seat in the house. The main dining area puts you within a few

The largest single brewing organization in the world is Anheuser-Busch Inc. of St. Louis, with 12 breweries in the United States. In 1990, the company sold 86.5 million barrels, the largest volume ever produced by a brewing company in a single year. The largest brewery on a single site is Coors Brewing Company in Golden, Colorado, which produced 597.99 million gallons of beer in 1990.

Beer was probably the original protein hair conditioner, and it works pretty well (thanks to the malto-dextrins and proteins). Try using German light lager, which is not too alcoholic. After shampooing, use the beer as a rinse, then let the hair dry (the protein should be left on the hair for a while so it can do its work). Later, comb the beer out if you want to, but the dried beer leaves no odor.

yards of the stage. Beyond that are low booths and a bar area that still provides a good view. The upstairs peanut gallery isn't bad either. The place is quite upscale, but not so staid that it isn't any fun. Jazz Alley has a long history in Seattle. It began as an alley-door place in the University District before moving downtown and poshifying itself. A few years ago, the club was remodeled, and now once again the entrance is in the alley. There is convenient garage parking nearby.

McCormick & Schmick's
1103 First Ave
623-5500
Mon-Fri 11 AM-11 PM, Sat 5 PM-11 PM, Sun 5 PM-10 PM

This downtown restaurant has an upscale saloon atmosphere, with dark wood, heavy glass, booths, and substantial furniture. A lot of the customers are downtown business people, either lunching (it's really busy at noon) or relaxing after work. Fashionwise, there's a bit of a Men's Wearhouse feeling about the place. The menu is solid American with an emphasis on seafood, and the microbrews are well-tended.

McCormick's Fish House and Bar
722 Fourth Ave
682-3900
Mon-Thurs 11 AM-11 PM, Fri & Sat 11 AM-midnight, Sun 5 PM-11 PM

At Fourth and Columbia, ever in the shadow of the lawyer-packed Columbia Center (the Darth Vader building), McCormick's has a fine bar and a business-suit crowd. As one guidebook put it, "Bankers like it because it looks like a bank." Many consider it the best of the downtown fish houses. It's always very busy at lunchtime, since it's right in the middle of the legal, business, and government district. It's full-service, with a good range of microbrews.

Shuckers (in the Four Seasons Olympic Hotel)

411 University St
621-1984
Mon-Thurs 11:30 AM-10 PM, Fri & Sat 11:30 AM-11 PM,
Sun 5 PM-10 PM

Shuckers is a pub and restaurant that features a health-conscious menu of Northwest seafood and an oyster bar that's considered by many to be the best in town. It specializes in microbrews, and has an attractive pub atmosphere with a full bar. You can sit outside in good weather.

PIKE PLACE MARKET

The Athenian Inn

1517 Pike Place
624-7166
Mon-Sat 6:30 AM-7 PM

Pike Place Market, Seattle's biggest tourist magnet, is a sprawling, noisy, colorful, multilevel, open-air, fresh-fish-and-vegetable, ethnic food, and crafts market, with restaurants and bars tucked under unlikely walkways. The long-running Athenian is an atmospheric bar and grill in the Pike Place Market

"Oh many a peer of England brews / Livelier liquor than the Muse, / And malt does more than Milton can / To justify God's ways to man."
—A. E. Housman, *A Shropshire Lad*

with spectacular views of Elliott Bay. There are 16 beers on tap, plus a wine-tasting bar, cocktails, and a soda fountain. A good seafood menu features prawns, scallops, salmon, clams, crab, halibut, squid, and more. Not to mention breakfast served all day.

Il Bistro
93 Pike St
682-3049
Daily 11:30 AM-2 AM

This informal, dark-wood Italian restaurant below street level in the elbow of the Pike Place Market never goes out of style. As with many spots in the Market, just finding Il Bistro makes you feel like you've somehow slipped behind the curtain and joined the in crowd. It's right beneath the main Market intersection, just under the big clock, but you have to slip around a railing and walk down a little ramp to find it. Go too far and you'll be wandering uncertainly down a wet brick alleyway. Il Bistro has nooks and crannies, white plaster and dark wood, a little jazz. On a busy night it's a fun place to just sit and watch the world drift by. It serves a few microbrews and offers a full bar and menu. The mussels are grand.

Kells
1916 Post Alley
682-1397
Daily 2 PM-2 AM

A lot of pubs aspire to Irishness, suggesting it by painting the walls green and playing The Chieftains and Van Morrison. It's not a bad idea. Seattle has a sizable Irish expatriate community, and non-Irish folks like to buy a little bit of the country at stores like Galway Traders in Ballard and Kells Irish Shop downtown. But Kells on Post Alley isn't merely Irishesque—it's Irish. It's a perfect place to wear the green on Saint Patrick's Day. Half of the place is a restaurant and bar, with a more raucous bar right next door, often featuring lively Irish music and always featuring stout and wee heavy. The biggest challenge is figuring out which bathroom is for men and which is for women—they're marked with some sort of ancient Irish terms.

Kells' area of the Market has a European flair. Right across the alley is an Italian bistro called The Pink Door, and nearby is Three Sisters, a bright yellow Continental sandwich shop. Another neighbor is a French crêperie run by a fellow who in another life was the guitarist for the Patti Smith group.

The Pink Door
1919 Post Alley
443-3241
Tues-Sat 11:30 AM-2 AM

You wander down an alley and step through an unmarked (but yes, pink) door. You find Italian food, weird entertainment, a rooftop terrace. Just a real cool place. At the Pink Door, you can eat in the dining room or sit in the bar and enjoy accordionist Tony Yazzolino or multipersonalitied cabaret entertainer Julie Cascioppo, whose act is like a Liza Minnelli acid flashback. The best seats, though, are on the patio in nice weather.

The Pink Door has an Italian feel, with a view of

"He that buys land buys many stones, / He that buys flesh buys many bones, / He that buys eggs buys many shells, / But he that buys ale buys nothing else."
—English proverb

"99 bottles of
beer on the
wall / 99 bottles
of beer / Take
one down / Pass
it around / 98
bottles of beer
on the wall."
—Drinking song

Elliott Bay and an occasional view of celebrities like regulars Ann and Nancy Wilson of Heart, or rock star Bonnie Raitt and author Tama Janowitz, who've been seen at the same table. (In fact, the Market is prime celeb territory. Sightings have included Yemenite singer Ofra Haza enjoying a solitary Thai chicken dinner, actor Dennis Hopper loitering on a bench near the Market Clinic, and our favorite: the apparently domesticated film legend Jean-Paul Belmondo buying an egg-slicer at the chic Sur La Table kitchenware store.)

Place Pigalle

81 Pike St
624-1756
Mon-Sat 11:30 AM-midnight

Not exactly a beer joint, this tiny (17 tables) restaurant and bar set in the elbow of the Pike Place Market was nevertheless one of the first places in Seattle to pour handcrafted ales. Place Pigalle specializes in microbrews and also has a full-service bar. The ambitious menu is fine, and the restaurant has fabulous views of Elliott Bay and the Olympics. It's bustling during the day when the clientele is business folks, shoppers, and tourists. It becomes candlelit and more subdued in the evening, when it's a romantic spot for lovers. There are outdoor tables in the summer months. As with just about everything else in the Market, good luck finding it. It's near the big clock—duck past the fish vendors and down a little hallway, out a door, in another door, and you're there.

The Virginia Inn

1937 First Ave
728-1937
Mon-Thurs 11 AM-1 AM, Fri 11 AM-2 AM, Sat noon-2 AM,
Sun noon-midnight

One of the most convivial pubs in town, the Virginia Inn has a European feel with a downtown and Market personality. It's in a great turn-of-the-century building where the Market meets Belltown. The VI has been in continuous operation since 1903. Artists, architects, and downtowners frequent the place in about equal numbers. The bar has a terrific selection of brews at all times, with seven microbrews and Guinness on tap. It also offers 12 wines by the glass and serves a pretty good bar menu of smoked salmon and jambon sandwiches. The brick walls are always hung with a changing exhibit of contemporary art, and the ambience is enhanced by good recorded music in a blues, jazz, adult-alternative mode. The VI is quiet in the afternoons and crowded after work and into the evening.

BELLTOWN

Casa-U-Betcha

2212 First Ave
441-1989
Daily 11:30 AM-1:30 AM

Abutting Pike Place Market to the north is Belltown, interchangeably referred to as The Regrade. The near-waterfront neighborhood runs roughly from the northern end of downtown to Seattle Center, with its epicenter at Second and Bell. A longtime studio district, it's being gentrified with high-rise apartments and condos, but it still retains a great deal of gritty ambience. There are more than 100 restaurants, cafes, and delis (I use the latter term loosely) in the area, as well as nightclubs, dance clubs, and various other attractions. Belltown is a fine place to simply sit and marvel at the variety of humanity.

Casa-U-Betcha is a trendy, youthful hangout with good Mexican food made with Northwest ingredients and an oddly angled, aluminum postmodern-Aztec decor that looks like it came from Dr. Caligari's workshop or Pee Wee's Playhouse. The full bar service includes a good selection of beer. Casa also has art exhibits, occasional live bands, and karaoke. At certain times of the day—prior to sundown, say, before the fashion vampires emerge—it can be a cool spot to sit and sip one. By night, Casa is jammed. It's on a stretch of street occupied by several dance clubs, including Downunder and Club Belltown. These places cater to college kids and people who've driven in from the Eastside looking for lively nightspots. They find them here, and Casa-U-Betcha is in the middle of it all.

Crocodile Cafe

2200 Second Ave
441-5611
Daily 7 AM-2 AM

When the Crocodile Cafe opened in 1991, it became an instant classic. It serves breakfast, lunch, and dinner to a clientele that's mixed and comfortable: older/younger, business types/artist types, stylish/rumpled. The main dining room has huge windows and Mardi-Gras-and-kitsch decor. Pineapple- or palm-leaf-shaped lampshades hang from the ceiling, festooned with colorful beads and little rubber crocodiles scurrying up and down the chains. The front window display might be an old yellow bicycle or Carl Smool's "Soft Seattle" fabric city skyline. The waiters are helpful and friendly, and the food is solid, gourmet All-American, such as grilled-cheese sandwiches topped with chanterelles in season. The Crocodile has a long microbrew list also.

All that would be enough to make the Crocodile a cool drop-in, but that ain't all. It also has a separate funky-chic cocktail lounge where people drag celebrities like David Byrne, Timothy Leary, and Eddie Van Halen when they're in town. And where local celebrities like Nirvana drag themselves when they're home. A largish booth-encircled back room is used for eclectic entertainment on weekend nights. The late-night amusements vary from the city's deftest singer-songwriters to furrow-browed folksingers, thumping reggae, and swirling jazz combos—with the occasional contortionist, sword-swallower, or limbo-dancer thrown in for variety. But these are the '90s, after all, so the main music menu is noisy modern

Beer—English
Bière—French
Bier—German
Cerveza—Spanish
Birra—Italian
Cerveja—Portuguese
Bere—Rumanian
Bier—Dutch
Öl—Swedish
Øl—Danish
Øl—Norwegian
Piwo—Polish
Pivo—Czech
Pivo—Serbo-Croat
Sör—Hungarian
Olut—Finnish
Bira—Turkish
Bir—Indonesian
Biero—Esperanto
Pivo—Russian
Bi'ra—Greek
Bira—Arabic
Birah—Hebrew
Bier—Yiddish
Biiru—Japanese
Pombe—Swahili
Zitos—Greek

bands. With most of them, you need an interpreter to explain their name, not to mention their lyrics. In other words, highly entertaining.

Dahlia Lounge
1904 Fourth Ave
682-4142
Mon-Fri 11 AM-10 PM, Sat & Sun 5:30 PM-11 PM

If you like food, you'll like the Dahlia Lounge. Chef Tom Douglas (who established Cafe Sport's reputation before going off on his own) is a regular, down-to-earth guy, but the meals he serves are exquisitely out of this world. His Dahlia Lounge is arguably the best restaurant in Seattle, yet the atmosphere is quite informal. Douglas likes to come out of the kitchen and chat with the customers, and the staff has a similarly relaxed but informed attitude. The interior of the place is bright red, with comfortable booths and fish-theme lamps. The music tends toward classic jazz and blues. There's also a full bar, including a fine complement of microbrews.

La Rive Gauche
2214 Second Ave
441-8121
Mon-Thurs 5 PM-11 PM, Fri & Sat 5 PM-1 AM

The beer list here is designed to enhance the menu and the ambience: French beers, some unusual Belgian beers, and a number of more conventional European brews. There is also an extensive wine list. Rive Gauche is a relaxed French bistro serving French regional specialties and homemade desserts, with live cocktail jazz or French cabaret music in the Edith Piaf mode on weekend nights. Even when there's no entertainment, the place has an appealing, linger-awhile atmosphere. It's sophisticated without being the least snooty, and the bartenders and waiters are very friendly. Owner, chef, and maître d' Jean-Paul Kissel serves the full menu (it's terrific) until midnight on weekends. The bistro is frequently busy, but seldom crammed, so seats are usually available.

The typical dinner customers are well-heeled and middle-aged or older; they've likely stopped in after an appetite-building evening at the theater. The other part of the crowd, usually found drinking or inhaling dessert at the bar, is younger—like the couple with complementary bleached flat-top hairdos, leather jackets, and faded jeans, sipping matching gin and tonics, or the two young men in modified smoking jackets and tortoise shell glasses staring gloomily into their cognacs.

The Two Bells Tavern

2313 Fourth Ave
441-3050
Mon-Fri 11 AM-2 AM, Sat & Sun noon-2 AM

This cozy Belltown tavern is a favorite of neighborhood artists, media types, and celebrities (Ann Wilson of Heart has put it on the top of her list of fave hangouts). The Two Bells has a few tables and booths crammed into a tiny space, a kitchen that is famous for the quality of its splendid soups and excellent potato salad, and the occasional bongos-and-poetry or strum-a-dum guitar entertainment. It's a congenial, bohemian setting for doing nothing

In California, it's against the law to enter a tavern on horseback. In Hawaii, you can't whistle in any place that serves drinks. In St. Louis, it's illegal for anyone but a working man to sit on a curb and drink beer from a bucket. In Natchez, Mississippi, the law prohibits cats "from drinking any beer whatsoever."

much while drinking a few microbrews (a few on tap and many intriguing bottled ones).

Writer Boy's Ditto
2305 Fifth Ave
441-3303
Daily 7 PM-midnight

Beer and poetry. I don't know how many brewers read poetry, but I know plenty of writers who enjoy a beer, and the Ditto provides a solid selection of microbrews. The Muse of Writing hovers over this little tavern on the fringe of Outer Belltown. The Monorail hovers over it, too. There are usually a few writers on hand, hard at their existential labors; the tavern has a copy machine and a few typewriters, in case paper and pencil aren't enough. At times the joint is swarming, especially on nights when Red Sky Poetry, a sort of writers' collective, holds its readings. These are the equivalent of musical open-mike nights: scribes and thinkers each take a turn declaiming from the stage. The Ditto also features jazz and new music from the cutting edge. Incidentally, the tavern is marked by one of the subtlest neon signs in the city, a little ditto (") mark.

In the United States, each person is allowed to homebrew up to 100 gallons of beer annually for personal enjoyment; the limit for a household of two or more adults is 200 gallons.

QUEEN ANNE / FISHERMEN'S TERMINAL

Chicago's

315 First Ave N
282-7791
Sun-Thurs 11:30 AM-10 PM, Fri & Sat 11:30 AM-1 AM

Chicago's is a squat, yellow one-story building on lower Queen Anne that sits directly across the street from the Seattle Center Coliseum. On nights when the SuperSonics are hosting an NBA opponent, the bar is a beehive for the couple of hours before tip-off; a lot of hoops fans use it as a meeting place, and quite a few return after the final buzzer to celebrate or to drown their sorrows. The restaurant and bar is surrounded by a sea of parking lots. Inside, Chicago's always seems a little dark, although there are spacious windows, including some wall-sized stained-glass pieces. The kitchen puts out decent Italian food. Blues and R&B groups rock the beat on weekends, so the bar is frequently lively even when the sports crowd is elsewhere.

Chinook's

1735 W Thurman St
(at Fishermen's Terminal)
283-4665
Mon-Fri 11 AM-10 PM,
Sat 7:30 AM-11 PM,
Sun 7:30 AM-10 PM

Fishermen's Terminal is the home port for the 700-odd boats in Seattle's fishing fleet. Visitors can walk up and down the piers, where fishermen are sometimes selling their catch right off the boat—and if they're not, the Wild Salmon fresh fish market always has delectable offerings.

Chinook's is a spacious seafood restaurant with a decor somewhere between Paris's Pompidou Centre and a warehouse: high, steel-beam ceilings and exposed ductwork. There are also a lot of terrific photos depicting the exciting, rugged fisherman's life. Almost all of the seats provide a good view of the boats docked outside. The atmosphere is informal and the food is top-quality. There's also a smaller takeout cafe adjacent to the main room.

Chinook's has full bar service in addition to its microbrew menu. The bar has seven taps specializing in microbrews, which make up 80 percent of the beer sales. Since the restaurant is so close to Fremont and Ballard, the biggest sellers are Redhook and Maritime. Chinook's makes beer-food matching suggestions on the menu, and holds an oyster festival in February that features beers to complement the oysters.

The Emerald Diner and Star Bar
105 W Mercer St
284-4618
Daily 8 AM-2 AM

The Emerald is a diner on lower Queen Anne that manages to be both arty and neighborly. The walls are watery-blue, the ceiling aqua, the booths and tables resplendent with the kind of blue-sparkle upholstery that once graced bicycle banana-seats. One wall has an underwater theme, with paintings of fish, crabs, and octopi. The opposite wall features geometric designs painted right onto the plaster. The nonsmoking (upper) and smoking (lower) sections are well separated by the bars, with table, booth, and horseshoe-bar seating. There's a full menu of American regional diner food.

At the rear of the spacious dining area is a tiny saloon called the Star Bar that features folk songwriters and jazz singers. It is purple, with a low ceiling lit up with star-points of light. Cocktails are available.

5 Spot

1502 Queen Anne Ave N
285-SPOT
Sun-Thurs 8:30 AM-10 PM, Fri & Sat 8:30 AM-11 PM

This restaurant serves good stylized American food, including regional specials. It's a pleasant space, right at the top of the Queen Anne Hillclimb (the Counterbalance) on upper Queen Anne. Big windows let in a lot of light, and the dining room includes both tables and booths. The little bar area, separated from the dining room by a low glass wall, is a pleasant place to drink a beer and have a conversation.

Highliner Tavern

1735 W Thurman St
(at Fishermen's Terminal)
283-2233
Daily 10 AM-midnight

The Highliner is on the waterfront and is usually half-filled with fishermen. It's basically just a big space with high metal beams in a fabricated building. But a visit to Fishermen's Terminal is always fun, and the Highliner in the early evening tends to be noisy and friendly. This is one of the bars where the fishermen themselves relax, so there's a casually raucous feeling in the air much of the time. A few pool tables are available, and a gigantic, silent TV screen is usually showing some obscure sports event, but most customers amuse themselves with conversation. You can get fish and chips from the grill.

Jake O'Shaughnessey's
100 Mercer St
285-1897
Daily 4:30 PM-2 AM

Jake's is famous for its Irish theme, its well-orchestrated liveliness, its substantial beer offerings, and its mountain of booze bottles stacked against the mirrored back bar. The place is boisterous, especially on nights when it's filled with revelers coming from or going to some event—sports, arts, or otherwise—at the nearby Seattle Center. There are occasional live music performances and comedy nights. The full-service kitchen specializes in Northwest cuisine. Jake's is in a building that is doomed for redevelopment one of these years, but in the meantime it is a saloon nonpareil.

Roadhouse
3407 Gilman Ave W
281-8379
Daily 10 AM-2 AM

The Roadhouse is on a diagonal arterial right next

to the Burlington Railroad yards in the low area called Interbay, between the hills of Magnolia and Queen Anne and just a few blocks from Fisherman's Terminal. The tavern serves a handful of microbrews and some solid homemade food. The place is ultra-informal, sometimes even rowdy, and the clientele is mostly residents of the nearby apartment complexes that have sprouted from the eastern Magnolia bluff like five-story mushroom gardens. The rest of the Roadhouse's customers are blues and jazz fans who come for the well-stocked jukebox and for the high-quality live music on weekends.

The Romper Room
106 First Ave N
284-5003
Sun-Thurs 4 PM-2 AM, Fri & Sat 4 PM-3 AM

The Romper Room dance club is one of the more unusual spots to have a beer. It's cultural mayhem at night, but during the day it can be a quieter spot. There's a drink-and-talk room next door, with art-lined walls, booths, and a pool table. A great deal of attention is given to the beers: several microbrews are always available, and a few new ones are often on tryout. The Romper Room turns up the volume late at night. Video screens flicker with old-fashioned videos or vintage rock music clips. Odd little half-doors line the walls, as if March Hares are about to come bursting in at any moment. There's also a heavy dose of ironic ersatz fishing imagery, fish nets, and ceiling-high tiki gods.

> "What will bring the effervescence, / Who will add the needed factor, / That the beer may foam and sparkle, / May ferment and be delightful?"
> —The *Kalevala* (an ancient folk epic of Finland)

T.S. McHugh's Public House

21 Mercer St
282-1910
Daily 11:30 AM-2 AM

McHugh's is a big, comfortable, sturdy restaurant and pub that appeals to the same customers that frequent its kitty-corner neighbor, Jake O'Shaughnessey's. They include arts and sports patrons who are on their way to an event at the Seattle Center or relaxing to talk it over afterward. The kitchen turns out Northwest and Irish cuisine. McHugh's also features Irish bands on weekends and on the occasional holiday.

Yukon Jack's

Seattle Center House
441-6600
Non-event nights 11:30 AM-6 PM, event nights (games or concerts) 11:30 AM-midnight

If you are a parent, sooner or later you are going to find yourself at the Center House for one of the wonderful exhibits, shows, or other activities that are put on for the tykes. The lower level houses the

Seattle Children's Museum. Outside the Center House are other Seattle Center attractions: the Space Needle, Pacific Science Center, the IMAX Theater, the Coliseum. Once you make sure that the little ones are well tended in some kind of chaperoned program—maybe a half-hour puppet show—you might sneak off to Yukon Jack's, located among all the other fast-food joints in the Center House's main atrium area. Oddly enough, this may be one of the most relaxing beers you'll ever have, especially in contrast to the general hyperactivity of the place.

> **"Payday came and with it beer."**
> **—J. Rudyard Kipling**

FREMONT / WALLINGFORD

The Buckaroo

4201 Fremont Ave
634-3161
Daily 11 AM-2 AM

What a joint. The 50-year-old Buckaroo joins the Comet and the Blue Moon in the triumvirate of majorly funky, enjoyably atmospheric drinkeries in town. The Buckaroo is a down-on-the-ground beer connoisseurs' place: it brings new meaning to the word "informal," but is entirely serious about beer. The bar always has a great selection of 16 beers on tap, many of them microbrews, and all of them well tended. Some are kept in special coolers and some are even tapped in arcane ways that enhance the flavor. The Buckaroo has a special faucet for stout that serves it "Dublin-style." It de-gasses the beer, leaving it velvet-smooth with a creamy head on top. It's the ultimate.

In America, a "pint" in a pub is usually a straight-sided glass holding 16 ounces (the British pint is 20 ounces). A "schooner" is usually a 10-ounce, slightly fluted glass.

Decor-wise, the Buck is hardly the ultimate, but it is unmatched, well-worn, and comfy. There are tables and booths, and two pool tables for recreation. The musical entertainment comes from a tape deck and a 400-tape selection.

The patrons tend to look slightly rough around the edges, but not intimidating. You suspect they aren't connoisseurs of much in life, but when it comes to beer, their taste is impeccable. The crowd is local Fremontians, drop-ins from around the city, and motor-cyclists who park their bikes on the sidewalk out front and stash their helmets in a special rack by the door.

The Buckaroo is in upper Fremont, up the hill from Fremont's main business district. You can't miss it—it's got a classic piece of neon that depicts a lasso-twirling cowboy on a bucking bronc.

Murphy's Pub
1928 N 45th St
634-2110
Daily 11 AM-2 AM

Murphy's, along with Cooper's, is responsible for much of Seattle's beer consciousness, both because of its longevity and because of its style. It specializes in Guinness ("The Ale You've Been Practicing For") and Northwest ales. For a decade or so, Murphy's was a narrow little tunnel of a storefront across from the Guild 45th movie theater in Wallingford. As if being narrow wasn't enough, the place was partly divided down the middle with a wall. It was like two hallways side-by-side, with a band crammed up in the window on the one side, and the patrons crammed every place else.

The "new" Murphy's opened in early 1992, on the corner a half-block west of the old address. (Just to show the way these things go, Murphy's took over the space of a defunct Radio Shack, and the old Murphy's is now a Starbucks.) It still has a green front with the name painted in the same lettering. In fact, many of the artifacts from the old location made the move down the street, including some etched glass in the front door and part of the bar itself. The room is large, square, and open, with windows all around looking out onto 45th. A big, double-sided fireplace stands solidly in the middle of the room.

While the layout of the pub is nothing like the old Murphy's, the personality is unchanged. They still serve some of the best beer in town, and the pub is still packed and lively. In fact, if there's a fault, it's that the place is too popular; it's standing room only most of the time, even on weeknights.

Pacific Inn
3501 Stone Way N
547-2967
Mon-Sat 11 AM-2 AM, Sun 3 PM-10 PM

This tiny tavern/cafe is not far from Gasworks Park, on a strip of street better known for its home fix-up, hardware, and paint stores. Well, after a hard day of comparison shopping for Venetian blinds, anybody could use a comforting drink. The Pacific Inn specializes in beer, plus great fish and chips. It's not much bigger than most living rooms, which means it's always comfortably intimate, and often jam-packed. Since it's right between Fremont and Wallingford, it draws from both neighborhoods.

The place changed owners a year or so ago (the new owner is Robert Julien, known to Seattle pub-goers for his longtime stint as the singing bartender at Jake O'Shaughnessey's), but nothing much has changed. The new bartenders are younger and have groovy haircuts; the CD jukebox still features Frank Sinatra, Robert Cray, and Buddy Holly. An added attraction: an actual parking lot surrounds the building. And there's a very cool sign, with a weird fish as the major element.

Ponti Seafood Grill

3014 Third Ave N
284-3000
Daily 11:30 AM-1 AM

Ponti is technically in the Queen Anne neighbor-hood, since it's along the southern bank of the Ship Canal, but it's just a block or so from Fremont. Tucked away at the south end of the Fremont Bridge, behind the more visible 318 Tavern and the Bleitz Funeral Home, this expensive, upscale restaurant specializes in exquisite seafood dishes. The tab for an evening's repast can be a bit unnerving, but the food is worth every hard-earned penny. The space is split into a couple of rooms, with nice views of the Ship Canal from nearly everywhere. There's also full bar service.

On weekend nights, Ponti is often noisily crammed with diners and scene-makers. In the afternoons, it's less hectic. In pleasant weather, the deck provides an excellent vantage point for lingering over a brew and gazing down at the boats motoring past. Right below the patio is a strip that is destined to become a canalside promenade and bicycle path.

Red Door Alehouse

3401 Fremont Ave
547-7521
Mon-Fri 11 AM-2 AM, Sat & Sun 11:30 AM-2 AM

Kitty-corner from the landmark sculpture and all-weather hat rack, *Waiting for the Interurban*—and within a block of two other good new pubs, the Dubliner and the Triangle—the Red Door Alehouse is popular with young professionals. Housed in a renovated building, the tavern is nice and clean and not too smoky, with 20 or so beers on tap, including many Northwest microbrews (available only in pitchers and pints, no schooners). The Red Door also has a wonderful menu, serving tasty sandwiches such as a grilled chicken breast.

The room itself is long, narrow, and high. Unlike most taverns, it's not cluttered with beeraphernalia. The dominant theme is historic Seattle, particularly the old fishing fleet. From the tables near the tall front windows, you can look out at the Fremont Avenue pedestrians and the traffic that backs up when the Fremont Bridge is raised to let boats pass by on the Ship Canal. The far end of the room opens out onto the Red Door beer garden, which is pleasant in warm weather. In fact, the knock on the Red Door has been that it's too new and too pleasant. But plenty of people like the atmosphere, so the Red Door has been a standing-room-only success ever since it opened. And in any event, the remedy for newness is to hang around for awhile; the Red Door gets more comfortably broken-in with each passing day.

Still Life in Fremont Coffeehouse

709 N 35th St
547-9850
Mon-Thurs 7:30 AM-
9 PM, Fri & Sat
7:30 AM-11 PM,
Sun 7:30 AM-9 PM

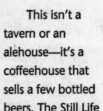

STILL LIFE IN FREMONT
COFFEEHOUSE

709 N 35½
SEATTLE, WA. 98103

547- 9850

This isn't a tavern or an alehouse—it's a coffeehouse that sells a few bottled beers. The Still Life makes great soups and other hearty, healthy food, and it has a living-room atmosphere with unmatched tables, easy chairs, changing art exhibits, and occasional live performances. Plus it's in Fremont, a neighborhood with a well-deserved reputation for choosing the bohemian approach to life. In good weather, the Still Life puts a few chairs out on the sidewalk. But good weather or bad, it's a comfortable place to shoot the breeze, write in a journal, or draw in a sketchbook. The Still Life is busy. It's all nonsmoking.

The 318 Tavern

318 Nickerson St
285-9763
Mon-Fri 11 AM-2 AM, Sat 11 AM-midnight

Just at the Queen Anne end of the Fremont Bridge (like Ponti Seafood Grill, it's actually on Queen Anne but feels like part of Fremont), the 318 serves Seattle's best burgers in a wedge-shaped little building at a busy five-way intersection. It's an unpretentious spot, and most of the customers come in for the burgers, beef stew, chili, and homemade fries. The clientele is extremely diverse, comprising workers of all kinds, a variety of ages, and people from the neighborhood. It's an easygoing place for a single person to drop in for a bite and a beer. For diversion, you'll find a pool table, pinball machines, and a CD jukebox.

UNIVERSITY DISTRICT / RAVENNA / ROOSEVELT

Blue Moon Tavern

712 NE 45th St
545-8190
Daily 12:30 PM-2 AM

No bar-crawl through Seattle would be complete

An Assyrian clay tablet relates that beer was taken aboard Noah's Ark, which, if you believe in it at all, is generally considered to have run aground in present-day Turkey.

without stumbling into the Blue Moon, just off I-5 at the edge of the University District, once the center of local intellectual life and a microcosm of the counterculture. Originally called the Big Dipper, the historically preserved legend has been operating continuously since 1934, the year Prohibition was repealed. Beatniks and Pulitzer Prize-winning poets alike have scrawled their graffiti on the bathroom walls (and not infrequently on the regular walls, for that matter) and carved their initials into the tables and booths.

As with most bars, you have to choose your moments at the Blue Moon. A civilized adult wouldn't really want to go there on a weekend night anymore, except as an anthropological field study. Its next-door neighbor is now a topless joint without booze, so the customers from that place have to slake their thirst somewhere. Otherwise, the tavern has hardly changed. Sunday night is Grateful Dead Night. Monday night is Opera Night. Tuesday night is Peanut Night. The rest of the nights are for people who don't like the Grateful Dead, opera, or peanuts.

The tavern opened at its present site in 1934 and, fraternity brawls aside, was fairly quiet for two decades. By the early 1950s, however, the Blue Moon had become a designated demilitarized zone where factions of Seattle's large and feisty Left could argue. "People went to the Blue Moon to drink and bullshit," says Walt Crowley, who helped prepare the tavern's landmark preservation petition. The petition called it "a haven from McCarthyism and Men in Gray Flannel Suits for left-wing activists such as Stan Iverson and William Cumming . . . and iconoclastic professors such as Victor Steinbrueck and Theodore Roethke."

During the 1950s, poet and University of Washington professor Theodore Roethke nurtured a school of writers who in turn nurtured the Blue Moon. When a messenger interrupted one of Roethke's lectures with the news that he had won Yale University's 1959 Bollingen Prize, the bard's response was "To the Moon!" There were times when four once-or-future Pulitzer Prize winners—Roethke, Stanley Kunitz, James Wright, and Carolyn Kizer— could be found drinking side by side at the bar.

In 1959, an article in the *Seattle Post-Intelligencer* described the Blue Moon's patrons as "night people" who had "already exiled themselves from the Poopdeck [a First Avenue tavern] because of the high tourist count. The beer is inexpensive, nothing is expected of them."

The Blue Moon has also served as a literary muse. Novelist Tom Robbins drew on it for passages in *Another Roadside Attraction* and called the tavern "a frenzy of distorted joy spinning just outside the reach of bourgeois horrors."

Its counterculture history aside, the Blue Moon is just about the only well-preserved example of the popular drinkeries that ringed the University District during the era when bars couldn't be within a mile of campus. In the late 1980s, the Moon survived a demolition threat. When developers wanted to raze it, the town rose up in defiance because of its storied beatnik past. It is now historically preserved on the basis of its history and ambience, not its architecture, and condos and offices will be built around it.

On its golden anniversary in 1984, the Blue Moon Tavern held a bathroom graffiti contest. The winning entry: "Some nights the wolves are silent and the moon howls."

College Inn Pub

4006 University Way NE
434-2307
Daily 2 PM-2 AM

The College Inn mixes English pub and University hangout, and both aspects benefit. One part of the basement pub features pool tables and similar entertainments. The back section is set up for drinking and talking, and the conversations tend to run to such topics as the nature of the universe. There are occasional poetry readings. There's also a smaller room that provides a measure of privacy for small groups. The customers are students, graduate students, foreign students. Most of these people have home, they have school, and then they have the College Inn Pub. The draft beers include nine micros, plus three imports. There's decent food, including soups, sandwiches, and pizza.

Duchess Tavern

2827 NE 55th St
527-0956
Mon 4 PM-2 AM,
Tues-Sat 11:45 AM-2 AM,
Sun 1 PM-10 PM
(10 AM-10 PM during football season)

The Duchess has been at the same location for 60 years. It's a onetime college hangout that has become more of a neighborhood tavern with a woody, 1960s charm. It was renovated a few years ago, so it has a more modern, spacious feel. The main clientele is neighborhood people, ex-UW students aged 30 to

55, sports enthusiasts and, still, lots of UW students. For diversion, there are pool tables, darts, pinball, a CD jukebox, cribbage and hearts tournaments, plus karaoke singing once a month. The kitchen turns out a solid pub-grub menu of salads, sandwiches, and soups. And there are 21 beers on tap, about half of them microbrews.

The Duchess is fondly remembered by UW grads of a certain era, when you had to roam a mile from campus to have a beer. There are several other similar drinkeries, and they have endured varying fates since changes in the law made them less vital destinations for thirsty students. The Red Robin, which began in 1943 as Sam's Red Robin Tavern next to the University Bridge, is now a franchise operation with restaurants up and down the West Coast. Another magnet for the counterculture of the 1960s and 1970s was the Century Tavern on University Way; one of the Seattle 7 was arrested there. Since 1987, it's been the University Sportsbar and Grill. A couple of other spots, though more distant from campus, belong to the same chapter of nostalgic history. The original Little Red Hen at 50th and Phinney was torn down in 1967 to make way for an apartment building. The Bounty, at Stone Way and Northeast 45th, has been replaced by a McDonald's. The Northlake Tavern was another bohemian hangout, but has been remodeled and is now known more as a family pizza place.

Pliny the Elder, in his *Natural History*, mentioned *cerevisia* as the national beverage of the Gauls.

**American Beer
Week is the first
full week in
October.**

Santa Fe Cafe
2255 NE 65th St
524-7736

and 5910 Phinney Ave N
783-9755
*Mon & Tues 5 PM-10 PM, Wed-Sat 11 AM-10 PM,
Sun 9 AM-10 PM*

The two Santa Fe Cafes serve what many
consider the city's best combination of food and beer,
with an excellent selection of the region's
microbrews. They led the way in popularizing
Southwestern cuisine in Seattle, and they remain
good places to eat (there's also a takeout-only outlet,
Blue Mesa, on upper Queen Anne Avenue). Spicy
food and beer go well together, and while Santa Fe's
food isn't terribly hot, the imaginative New Mexico-
style menu works well with the robust ales. The decor
in both locations is pleasant, with a nice bar for
people who are waiting to be seated or who are just
enjoying a drink and chitchat.

Teddy's Off Roosevelt
1012 NE 65th St
526-9174
Mon-Fri 3 PM-2 AM, Sat & Sun 1 PM-2 AM

Teddy's is a neighborhood tavern in the
Roosevelt area a mile north of the University District.
It's a pleasant, often quiet spot with a few plants
hanging in the front windows, pool tables, darts,
video games, and pinball machines. It serves both

microbrews and import beers. The bar has outdoor seating in a beer garden during the summer, as well as outdoor Ping-Pong (and if you haven't seen bar patrons trying their hand at Ping-Pong, you've got to check it out). Teddy's also has an extensive selection of tapes and CDs.

CAPITOL HILL

Comet Tavern
922 E Pike St
323-9853
Daily noon-2 AM

The Comet is amiably scruffy. That's precisely the reason why it is the favorite bar of many beer-drinkers. The proprietors are not into shiny furniture, performance art, a high-pressure social scene, or inventive food. At the Comet, they care about their beer and about providing a casual atmosphere for tipping a few and carrying on a conversation. The Comet has character. It's the kind of noisy place where unsuspecting first-time customers hesitate as they walk through the door—their eyes dart around and their first instinct is to back out. Two hours later, they are enjoying themselves and understand why somebody recommended the cheerful, unpretentious spot in the first place.

Roanoke Park Place Tavern
2409 10th Ave E
324-5882
Mon-Sat 11:30 AM-2 AM, Sun noon-midnight

This lively north Capitol Hill sports bar attracts customers from the neighborhood as well as University types who venture over the bridge. But the clientele is eclectic: lawyers, punks, working people. It's sports-oriented, not so much in decor but because the pub sponsors teams in lacrosse, soccer, basketball, volleyball, ultimate frisbee, darts, ping-pong, baseball, and skiing. Almost all conversations are high-decibel. A space off the main bar provides a somewhat cozier chatting area. The tavern specializes in microbrews, and the menu runs to salads, sandwiches, and similar pub grub.

MADISON PARK / LESCHI

The Attic
4226 E Madison St
323-3131
Daily 11 AM-2 AM

The Attic has a high, open-beamed ceiling and big windows that look out onto a quiet stretch of Madison, where car traffic is slowed by traffic diverters. Skylights add to the bright feeling of the place during the day. The Attic isn't fancy, just comfortable. Padded benches line the gray brick walls, and the rest of the seating is scarred wooden chairs that look used but not used up. During the day, the customers are a mix of ages and styles, drinking microbrews and talking under posters for Samuel Adams ale. The Attic serves sandwiches, chili, and breakfasts on Sunday. There are the usual diversions, such as darts, and on weekend nights bands come in and play on a little stage at the back.

Leschi Lakecafe

102 Lakeside Ave S
328-2233
Daily 11:30 AM-midnight

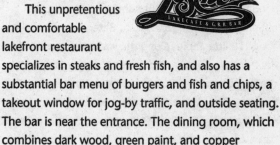

   This unpretentious and comfortable lakefront restaurant specializes in steaks and fresh fish, and also has a substantial bar menu of burgers and fish and chips, a takeout window for jog-by traffic, and outside seating. The bar is near the entrance. The dining room, which combines dark wood, green paint, and copper accents, is lined with windows that provide panoramic views of Lake Washington, a marina right below the restaurant, the Cascades, the taller buildings of Bellevue, the I-90 bridge, and Mount Rainier. In the summer, there's a beer garden.
   After 10 years in business, the Leschi Lakecafe was recently refurbished. The clientele includes neighborhood people, lots of families, boaters, joggers, and bicyclists (the cafe is near Madrona Park and Lake Washington Boulevard).

"Simple pleasures are the last refuge of the complex."
—Oscar Wilde

Red Onion Tavern
4210 E Madison St
323-1611
Daily 11 AM-2 AM

The Red Onion is a typical example of the way microbrews have seeped into Seattle bar culture. It's in an area of Madison Park that was an amusement park around the turn of the century and is now populated by restaurants, wine shops, cheese shops, bakeries, boutiques, interior decor shops, and cafes. The Red Onion is just a regular bar, with just a handful of beers on tap. But included among the offerings is the *de rigeur* Ballard Bitter. The Onion has about 10 little tables along the wall, a few booths in the front windows, and a bunch of larger tables that can be pushed together in front of a huge open fireplace. These always seem to be occupied by noisy soccer teams. There are a few entertainments in the bar: a couple of pool tables, and a sign announcing "Red Onion Dominoes Tournament." But for the most part, the patrons are there to drink and talk, and the place is lively with conversation.

BALLARD / GREENWOOD / PHINNEY RIDGE

Crosswalk Tavern
8556 Greenwood Ave N
789-9691
Mon-Sat 10 AM-2 AM, Sun 10 AM-midnight

The Crosswalk is a regular sports bar, with posters of James Worthy and Michael Jordan and enough Husky paraphernalia to keep the UW athletic department solvent until the turn of the century. It has red-topped booth tables and upholstered seats with the stuffing coming out here and there. There are also some longer tables toward the back, so you can come in with 8 or 10 people and not have to hassle with shoving tables together. The CD jukebox might well be playing Dwight Yoakam or Neil Young. ("Is it too loud?" "Country music's always too loud.") The Crosswalk serves an adventurous pizza menu, with the pizza chef right there manning the ovens by the door. On tap are eight or so microbrews.

Hiram's At The Locks
5300 34th Ave NW
784-1733
Mon-Thurs 11 AM-10 PM, Fri-Sun 11 AM-10:30 PM

One of the great pleasures of Seattle life is watching the parade of boats on the Ship Canal. There are few more satisfying ways to productively waste an afternoon than to sit idly canalside while the weekend sailors slip past. Pack a sandwich, a bottle of beer, a book, a notebook and pen, and find a spot along the canal anywhere from Fremont to the

Hiram M. Chittenden Locks. Sit around for a couple of hours doing nothing much and see if your well-being isn't enhanced. If you're not in the mood to pack a knapsack, Hiram's is a fine alternative, with good food, good beer, and grade-A views of the canal from outdoor umbrella tables or indoor picture windows. Just west of the locks, Hiram's is a prime spot for watching the maritime activity, in an unpretentious corrugated green metal building that one reviewer described as belonging to the grain-silo school of architecture.

La Boheme Tavern
6119 Phinney Ave N
783-3002
Daily 11 AM-2 AM

LaBo's motto is "Enjoy darts, pool, and good conversation in a pub-like atmosphere." First opened in 1934, it's in one of Seattle's more distinctive buildings, which looks like a one-bedroom chateau. On the inside, it's about the size of an efficiency apartment (the official capacity is 49), with a pool table crammed in at one end. The 20 beers on tap include lots of microbrew ales, but you'll still see neighborhood pensioners sipping at cans of Olympia.

La Boheme has plenty of personality, but not so much that a newcomer will feel uncomfortable. At least half of the people in there seem to know each other—the garrulous old guys in gimme caps at the bar drinking Ballard Bitter; a couple of talkative bowling-league ladies working on the bar's white wine supply; two stout young men in overalls and beatnik goatees enthusing over Black Butte, an exotic ebony stout from Oregon. But all of these patrons, instead of gazing suspiciously at newcomers, are glad to include a stranger in their conversation.

The decor is similarly unique: a steep-sloped ceiling, red curtains, stuffed deer heads, some pre-vintage Hamm's and Olympia advertisements, a copy of Manet's *Olympia* hanging over the bar, and a bulletin board with yellowing newspaper clippings about La Boheme. It's the kind of place where the men's room is marked "Gents," with no sense of quaintness. And it's so intimate, shall we say, that if you sit on the last stool at the bar you're in danger of periodic nudging from a cuestick. There's also a dart board tucked into an opposite corner, and patrons can check out Trivial Pursuit, backgammon, chess, checkers, and Scrabble, not to mention an argument-settling library of volumes including the *World Almanac.*

New Melody

5213 Ballard Ave NW
782-3480
Daily 2 PM-2 AM

Ballard will probably never escape its role as the butt of all civic jokes—the not-with-it neighborhood that never-will-be. The rest of Seattle is busily tooling around in a red Mazda Miata, or at least a Volvo station wagon, while Ballard still cruises slowly in a brown Buick bulgemobile, unfastened seatbelt dangling out the closed driver's-side door. Ballard pulls out right in front of you and then, oblivious,

"I have a total
irreverence for
anything
connected with
society, except
that which
makes the road
safer, the beer
stronger, the old
men and women
warmer in winter
and happier in
summer."
—Brendan Behan

immediately stops to hang a left. But, unlikely as it
might seem and uneasy as it might make comedians,
Ballard has the densest agglomeration of nightclubs
outside of downtown. And these are not Nordic
nightspots filled with rampaging Swedish housewives
cranked on lutefisk and lefse, twitching maniacally to
the polkaholic wheezing of Stan Boreson imper-
sonators. Within a block or two of the New Melody
are several other nightspots, including the Backstage,
Seattle's premier music nightclub for adults.

The New Melody is a large tavern with an eclectic
music schedule. It's mainly known as a folk and
bluegrass spot, but it also regularly hosts Cajun
bands, adventurous acoustic songwriters, and jazz—
from alarming bang-on-a-can improvisation to warm-
milk big band swing. The New Melody's high ceiling
and big front windows give it a capacious feel. The
walls are hung with vintage musical instruments. It's
set up as two rooms, with a wall running halfway
down the middle, though you can see the stage from
nearly anywhere. One side has a pool table and the
bar. The other holds the stage, dance floor, and
tables. There are usually several microbrews on tap.
Hey, free popcorn, too.

The New Melody is on a little diagonal side street
called Ballard Avenue. Heads up, because—leave it to
Seattle—this intersection seems to have been
designed by Rubik. Ballard Avenue is between 22nd
and 24th, and there's no 23rd, of course. The avenue
doesn't even cross Market; it just turns onto it from
the south side. To muddle things even further, it's a
one-way street right there (it turns into two-way just a
block down), so to get there you have to drive around
the block and weave through a couple of back streets.

It's actually more confusing to describe than to navigate, and there are payoffs. Because other businesses in the neighborhood close down at the end of the day, there's always plenty of free parking.

The Old Pequliar

1722 NW Market St
782-8886
Daily 11 AM-2 AM

The Old Pequliar is an Irish pub. No jokes about the name, now. And after all, it could have been "Ye Olde" Pequliar. (Actually, the name comes from a type of British beer.) In any event, this alehouse, which replaced the old Valhalla Tavern in 1991, has a green front (always a good sign) with yellow and rust trim. Inside, the room is wider than it is long, with a scuffed yellow concrete floor, a color scheme heavy on oak and green, and walls bedecked with hunting scenes.

Six or eight microbrews are on draft behind the long bar, and the friendly bartender will serve up a short sample of any unfamiliar brews. The Old Pequliar sells more Guinness than any other bar in Washington state. The clientele is about 60 percent expatriate Irishpersons, with the rest of the crowd made up of young couples and neighborhood Ballardites. Cigarettes are much in evidence.

The furnishings include an array of comfortable wooden chairs and tables, deep-green bar stools, and upholstered benches along the white-curtained front windows. There's a gaudy CD jukebox, a pool table, darts, electronic darts, and the occasional Irish music session. The most charming feature of The Old

Pequliar is a little nook with easy chairs and a well-stocked bookcase that encourages reading and literary chitchat.

The Owl Cafe

5140 Ballard Ave NW
285-3640
Mon-Fri 11:30 AM-2 AM, Sat & Sun 7 PM-2 AM

The Owl is a blues bar. Neither eclectic nor self-conscious, it looks like it's been around forever, with live blues, R&B, or jazz every night of the week. The decor is classic Seattle-brick-wall with music-theme paintings, including big portraits of blues legends Memphis Minnie and Little Walter hanging watchfully over the stage. The music fits a format, but the crowd does not. It's a mix of ages and races. The chicness level ranges from pretty cool to pretty hopeless.

The ambience is friendly, loud, smoky, beery, and fun.

The Owl is a quiet jazz cafe by day, serving a Cajun menu. But by midnight Saturday, the place is crammed. The bands tend to be good, in a workhorse, bar-band way. Blues is the most individual expression of the most universal emotions; it's about life. It's easily commanded on a superficial level, but true mastery comes from deep within. There's nothing better than a good blues band, nothing worse than a bad one. The bands that play at the Owl are not perfect, but they're perfect for the time and place.

74th St. Alehouse

7401 Greenwood Ave N
784-2955
Sun-Thurs noon-midnight, Fri & Sat noon-2 AM

The emphasis is on good beer, good food, and good atmosphere at this lively, slightly upscale neighborhood alehouse on the fringe of the Greenwood antique-store district, not far from the Woodland Park Zoo and Green Lake. Announced by a prominent neon sign, the 74th St. Alehouse has vast storefront windows opening onto Greenwood Avenue. The narrowish interior is open and bright, with light walls, stained glass, big admiring photos of British pubs, and wooden tables and chairs.

On a typical Friday evening, the alehouse is relaxed and enjoyably noisy with talk. The tables are filled with cheerful, regular-looking baby boomers, the TVs might be showing a Sonics basketball game with the sound off, and music plays on the fine sound system (although you usually can't hear much of it over the conversational racket). It's not too smoky. If conversation isn't enough, there are two regulation steel-tip dart boards.

The alehouse is beer-oriented, with 16 draft ales and lagers, including a number of specials and specialty brews announced on a chalkboard. The waiters are all friendly and helpful, and the bartenders will gladly pull a one-sip cup of any unfamiliar but intriguing offering. All of the local microbrews are available, as are a changing roster of imports such as John Courage Amber Ale and Abbott Ale. The kitchen produces a pleasing fresh-food menu that includes clam chowder, seafood gumbo, hot pastrami

"Beer is the Danish national drink, and the Danish national weakness is another beer."
—Clementine Paddleford in the *New York Herald Tribune*, June 20, 1964

sandwiches, Italian sausage sandwiches, and filberts oven-roasted in rosemary and butter.

The Sloop

2830 NW Market St
782-3330
Daily 11 AM-2 AM

The Sloop, one of Ballard's best taverns, is near the Locks and on the way to Shilshole Bay, so it's a good place to stop when you're in the maritime mood. It was the first tavern in Seattle to pour Ballard Bitter, so it was in on the very beginnings of the microbrew revolution. A few other microbrews are always on tap. It's really just a terrific specimen of a regular bar. You can drink a beer and have a conversation, or just sit and enjoy life. The Sloop serves a little pub grub and has a pool table and dart boards.

GREEN LAKE / MAPLE LEAF / WEDGWOOD / LAKE CITY

Cooper's Northwest Ale House

8065 Lake City Way NE
522-2923
Mon-Fri 3 PM-2 AM, Sat 1 PM-2 AM, Sun 1 PM-midnight

Cooper's, with 22 taps, is a mecca for Seattle beer connoisseurs and a flagship of the local movement, billing itself as "Seattle's Original Ale House." The only negative thing about Cooper's is getting there. It's right on Lake City Way, a traffic-packed arterial. Coming from the direction of downtown, you're prohibited from making a left turn when you see the alehouse's sign, so you're likely to sail right past and find yourself driving around endless side streets. It's typically Seattle: you can't get right over there from here.

That's the end of the bad news, though, because once you get there, Cooper's is a comfortable place that somehow manages to have a small-pub atmosphere in a pretty big room. The dress code runs to tweeds, jeans, anoraks, down vests and, on the men anyway, a higher percentage of beards than in the general population. The staff is easygoing, down-to-earth, and very knowledgeable about beer. They'd better be, considering the clientele: "Welcome Guinness Society Members" is a not-uncommon message on the inside readerboard.

The decor nods to rowing, with a pair of oars hanging on one wall. When there are big crew events in town, Cooper's tends to fill up with healthy, strong oarspersons. All pubs that imagine they are capturing a little bit of England have dart boards, but Cooper's goes them better, with four elaborate dart-tossing lanes, announcements of league standings, and even a dart-on-a-pedestal trophy. The music is never intrusive, but always loud enough to catch your interest, especially since it's always hip, tending to blues, R&B, and other roots-oriented sounds. Similarly, there are TVs, but they're on only for big games and other major events. And in the category of little things that make Cooper's pleasant, it's not as smoky as some bars. Cooper's also serves food, specializing in beer-battered fish and chips and other better-than-typical tavern fare.

The folk wisdom that you shouldn't drink too much on an empty stomach is valid. Food in the stomach slows the absorption of alcohol into the bloodstream.

Latona Tavern

6423 Latona Ave NE
525-2238
Mon-Fri 3 PM-1 AM, Sat 1 PM-2 AM, Sun 2 PM-2 AM

This small, high-ceilinged, young professionals'
spot is light-filled, with big windows that look out on
65th Street and nearby antique shops. The interior
has sponge-painted walls and teal columns behind
the bar, plus nice slate-topped tables. The Latona
really pays attention to microbrews, and several
specialties are always on tap. A tiny kitchen turns out
soups, sandwiches, and nachos. In the off-hours, it's a
pleasant, well-lit spot to have a chat or do a little
paperwork.

The Latona is also known for its musical
programming, with a little stage stuck near the far
end of the room. The entertainment runs to folky
singer-songwriters and easy jazz. When it's busy, the
Latona is pretty lively with both conversation and
music. Although the clientele tends to be fairly
homogeneous, the people-watching is still good. You
might see a woman in a beret smoking a long, skinny
brown cigarette. Or you might see a couple get up
and slow-dance unselfconsciously when a jazz trio
plays "Stardust."

Maple Leaf Grill

8909 Roosevelt Way NE
523-8449
Mon-Fri 11:30 AM-10 PM, Sat 4 PM-10 PM

The Maple Leaf Grill combines three influences:
New Orleans, music, and microbrews. It's a small,

restored 1930s tavern with four or five booths and seating for a dozen at the bar. The decor hints at Art Deco in the design of the back bar and the lamp fixtures. Stylish framed paintings of musicians hang on the walls over the booths. The Maple Leaf serves a very interesting menu of beer-friendly food—burgers, heavy fries, fish stews, breaded catfish—as well as six or eight microbrews. Call ahead for a booth.

Wedgwood Draft House & Cafe

8515 35th Ave NE
527-2676
Mon-Fri noon-midnight, Sat 8 AM-midnight,
Sun 8 AM-2 PM

Fourteen craft beers are on tap at this nice little beer-oriented neighborhood spot. Don't be surprised if you hear customers knowingly discussing several of them with the chatty, pleasant owner and bartender. The Wedgwood is in a small residential/business district with a few grocery stores, banks, and small shops. Tables and booths hug the walls, but the windows look out onto 35th Avenue and there is a considerable open space separating the eating areas from the horseshoe bar. The chow includes seafood, steak, pasta, and sandwiches for lunch and dinner, as well as breakfast on weekends. The place is more oriented toward eating in the early evening, then takes on more of a bar atmosphere in the later hours. Since Wedgwood isn't exactly in the heart of the city, or on the way to or from anyplace, the Draft House has a neighborhood feel.

WEST SEATTLE

Luna Park Cafe
2928 SW Avalon Way
935-7250
Daily 7 AM-10 PM

This friendly spot, combining neighborliness and kitsch, is tucked under the West Seattle Bridge, just barely into West Seattle. Take the exit just past Harbor Island, long before the freeway reaches West Seattle proper. The Luna Park serves only a few beers, but it is always a comfortable place to linger over a brew. The selection is typically something like a Ballard Bitter and a Full Sail Ale, along with the occasional seasonal special, such as Snow Cap Ale. A range of commercial bottled beers is also on the menu.

The cafe is decorated with vintage pop-culture stuff, including advertising signs from Seattle businesses of the past. This aesthetic is shared by many cafes and bars, but at the Luna Park it doesn't feel the least bit affected or self-conscious.

Salty's on Alki
1936 Harbor Ave SW
937-1600
Mon-Thurs 11 AM-9:30 PM,
Fri & Sat 11 AM-10:30 PM,
Sun 9:30 AM-9:30 PM

Salty's has the best view of the Seattle skyline except the one from an incoming ferry. Naturally, it's best on hot summer days, when the deck is a prime place to be. But of course, on hot summer days lots of other people will have the same idea, so it will be plenty crowded. Besides the look at Seattle's ever-changing profile (and it's a pretty terrific-looking town, in case you haven't checked it out lately), you might get a glimpse of the oceangoing ships and the colorful shapes of industrial machinery on nearby Harbor Island.

Salty's is a well-appointed restaurant and a good place to throw a party or hold a reception, thanks to the dramatic panorama. Even when there's not a formal party going on, the restaurant sometimes approaches partylike activity levels. Salty's also has a branch on Redondo Beach (north of Federal Way) and another on the Commencement Bay waterfront in Tacoma.

Eastside

BELLEVUE

The New Jake's
401 Bellevue Square
455-5559
Daily 11 AM-11 PM

The New Jake's is a variation on the theme of restaurant-and-bar spots invented by the team of Tim Firnstahl and Mick McHugh. The two have split up, but even most of their separate spots—from Jake O'Shaughnessey's to the Kirkland Roaster to The Roost—have the feel of their combined efforts. This one does, too. When you just can't shop another minute, drop in. The food is good, there's a full bar, and it's beer-oriented, with 28 brews that range from Bud Light to Pete's Wicked Ale.

The Pumphouse
11802 NE Eighth St
455-4110
Mon-Sat 7 AM-midnight

You can tell that the Pumphouse is a popular joint because all of the nearby businesses have "No Pumphouse Parking" signs in front of their own parking spaces. The Pumphouse, right off busy Northeast Eighth, is a small, unassuming bar with a long menu of pub grub, a good selection of beers, helpful employees, and a friendly crowd of mixed ages comprising workers, business people, and often local politicians.

Don't be surprised to hear great Motown oldies on the sound system. In every way, the Pumphouse is comfortably worn, without being worn out. The room has big windows, but it has a dark feel, with wood walls and big, rough-hewn posts. The busy kitchen turns out a menu that tends toward barbecue burgers. The beer, including several microbrews, is served in pitchers, one-liter steins, and mugs.

FACTORIA

Factoria Pub
Factoria Square
643-4229
Mon-Thurs 10 AM-midnight, Fri & Sat 10 AM-2 AM

Here's a regular shopping-mall pub for young people, like scores of others around the area, but with a selection of microbrews on tap and lots of diversions. Just inside the front door are several electronic dart boards; beyond are a handful of pool tables and the bar. On a busy Friday night all of the areas are filled and busy with activity. The decor is brick and wood, but obscured by all kinds of commercial beer advertising.

KIRKLAND

Kirkland Roaster & Ale House

1111 Central Way
827-4400
Daily 11:30 AM-2 AM

This is one of the formula Firnstahl/McHugh spots, which went to Firnstahl when the partners divvied up their empire. It's an informal, slightly upscale drinkery and restaurant on a near-waterfront street in downtown Kirkland. It's snuggled between a winery on one side (Covey Run) and a brewery on the other (Hale's Ales). In fact, you can look through the windows of the Roaster right into Hale's and see the shiny tanks and watch the brewing process. This gives the feel of a brewpub, even though the two businesses aren't formally associated (the Roaster does serve Hale's ales, of course).

The interior is comfortably classy: dark wood, green half-curtains on the front windows, wooden chairs, and pounded-copper tables illuminated by hanging lamps with dark purple shades. Onto that

"St. George
he was for
England / And
before he killed
the dragon / He
drank a pint of
English ale / Out
of an English
flagon."
—G. K. Chesterton,
The Englishman

backdrop, the decorator has thrown the now-familiar overload. To name just a few of the things stuck to the walls: beer trays, framed beer labels and logos, artfully arranged beer taps, wine bottle displays, and for good measure, a handful of Seahawks-theme collages and a framed Steve Largent football uniform.

Had enough? Hanging from the ceiling are microbrewery pennants: a black flag with a gold pyramid for Pyramid Ales, the purple and gold oval of Thomas Kemper, and many more. The beer theme is backed up by the 19 beers on tap, including many microbrews and specialty beers.

Smokie Jo's Tavern
106 Kirkland Ave
827-8300
Mon-Fri 3 PM-2 AM, Sat & Sun 11 AM-2 AM

Jo Dooley's tavern serves a good selection of draft beers in an unpretentious, laid-back atmosphere. It's a neat, cozy bar that caters mostly to neighborhood people and beer lovers. Most of the customers amuse themselves with conversation, but there are also pool tables, darts, video games, and a jukebox.

Yarrow Bay Bar & Grill
1270 Carillon Point
889-9052
Daily 11:30 AM-9:30 PM

This waterfront restaurant, with a view of Seattle across Lake Washington, has both a formal dining room and a more casual cafe area. The menu is diverse and fairly health-conscious. The restaurant itself has dark-wood booths, and the walls are adorned with Edward Curtis photos. Downstairs on the deck (this is called the Beach Cafe), the view of the city is quite dramatic, especially at sunset. All of the booths provide a nice view. Although this spot is on the waterfront and the address is Kirkland, don't mistake it for the casual atmosphere of downtown Kirkland. It's in the swanky Carillon Point development, so even the informality of the Beach Cafe is somewhat upscale.

ISSAQUAH

The Roost
120 NW Gilman Blvd
392-5550
Mon-Thurs 11:30 AM-9 PM, Fri & Sat 11:30 AM-10 PM,
Sun 10 AM-10 PM

What could be better than a restaurant with 22 beers on tap *and* you get served by a giant rooster? Actually, this is a place to take the kids, with kid food and kid diversions. On Wednesdays, kids under 12 eat free from a special children's menu; on other days, there are various other deals and all-you-can-eat specials for adults, too. The Roost is also a good place for nonparents to visit, just to see what this other world is all about. It's like a "Calvin and Hobbes" comic strip magnified about a million times. They spill, they dribble, they throw stuff, they spin around and around. They laugh, they cry. The Scream-o-meter doesn't go high enough to measure the noise level. Since kids (other people's kids) are hilarious, the

Roost on Wednesdays is highly entertaining. You'll
find booster chairs, coloring paper and crayons, toys,
and a window you can look through to watch the
cooks at work. Adults? Just eat, drink a beer, and stay
out of the way.

MERCER ISLAND

Roanoke Inn
1825 72nd Ave SE
232-0800
Mon-Sat 11 AM-2 AM, Sun noon-midnight

Take a wrong turn off I-90 and you could easily
find yourself driving all over Mercer Island. Even if you
take the right turn, you could miss it, because the
Roanoke Inn is in an inconspicuous little house in
what seems to be a residential neighborhood. It's not
your stereotypical Mercedes Island place; it's a regular
bar. There are a bunch of booths, some of them
upholstered in an odd, faded-orange color. There are
vintage lampshades with nature scenes, and a ton of
beer stuff, most of it in the Spuds McKenzie genre. To
the back is a little wood-paneled room with a pinball
machine. Down a hallway is another little room with a
pool table. There are a couple of front-porch tables,
for use when the weather is pleasant. You can get a
bowl of tomato soup or a Reuben sandwich, and
while the Roanoke doesn't specialize in microbrews, it
does serve a few. If you're there in the afternoon,
you're liable to share the space with a handful of old
regulars.

North

EDMONDS

Mick Finster's Pub & Grill

24001 Hwy 99
775-2121
Daily 11 AM-2 AM

If you get thirsty driving north on Aurora, you might want to swing in to Mick Finster's, a sports bar and cardroom just across the Snohomish County line, next to the Burlington Coat Factory outlet. Finster's is the kind of place with sports-team pennants hanging all over, the kind of place with a cardroom, the kind of place where you shouldn't be surprised to see a guy in a down vest and a golf hat swigging a bottle of Coors Lite. But there're also Redhook and Pyramid, friendly waiters, and a decent menu in the tuna melt and clam chowder mode.

LAKE FOREST PARK

Lake Forest Inn Roadhouse

18018 61st Ave NE
486-8021
Mon-Fri 2 PM-2 AM, Sat & Sun noon-2 AM

Ordinarily, it's not a good sign when you order a schooner and the bartender asks, "You mean a little one?" But the Lake Forest Inn Roadhouse is actually a most convivial place to spend a quiet afternoon drinking Hale's Wee Heavy and watching pro football playoffs on the big-screen TV. The tavern is in Lake Forest Park, way up at the northern end of Lake Washington. It features 15 taps, mostly pouring commercial beers but also a handful of micros, including some nice ones like the aforementioned Wee Heavy and Redhook's winter warmer, called Winterhook.

The bar has a few big windows, but they are kept pretty well covered, so the place is only slightly better lit than the Carlsbad Caverns. Besides the little bit of daylight squeaking in through the blinds, there's a dab of neon and a few lantern-style lampshades hanging above the bar. Three pool tables sit right near the front door, there's a recessed dance floor (for dancing on Friday and Saturday nights), lots of tables with comfortable padded chairs, and a back area loaded with dart boards.

The afternoon crowd is mixed, a handful of 25-ish guys with slightly out-of-date hairstyles and the beginnings of beer bellies; a few older guys, one of them wearing a golf hat; a young woman in a black vinyl windbreaker and the kind of big hair that would draw stares in town, but here nobody bats an eye.

Gardeners know the value of beer as a weapon against slugs. At night, set out a few saucers of beer around your garden, or half-bury a bottle at an angle, with some beer in the bottom. Slugs are like people—they love beer. But also, like some people, once they get into the brew, they never get out. In the morning, check the saucers and dispose of the sodden slugs.

WOODINVILLE

Armadillo Barbecue
13109 NE 175th St
481-1417
Daily 11 AM-10 PM

The Armadillo is a little cinder-block place in a mini-strip-mall, with a big black armadillo silhouette on the front. The kitchen is right inside the front door and it smells smoky from the barbecue; there's the clatter of dishes and the sound of Motown. "Ribs Is The Answer," promises a sign.

The walls are covered with Americana. The overall theme is armadillo and cactus, supplemented by African masks and big ceramic cow heads. Some of

it is funny semi-kitsch, some of it is just weird. There are tables of all sizes, for groups from two to a dozen or so, plus a handful of booths. It's a comfortable place, busy at noon and in the evening, both at the tables and at the takeout counter. There are always a half-dozen or so microbrews on tap. But the big attraction, obviously, is the barbecue, which is served in full dinners and in sandwiches (there's chicken, if the idea of pork and beer is just too much). As the waiter asked, "You want the killer hot sauce?"

West

BAINBRIDGE ISLAND

Four Swallows

4569 Lynwood Center Rd NE
842-3397
Daily 5 PM-9 PM

The Four Swallows is a five-minute drive from the Bainbridge ferry dock. Stop by the Visitor Information Center for a map and directions. As an added benefit, the route provides a brief look at the island lifestyle. You'll also pass an impressive, well-weathered barn. The Four Swallows itself is in a small Tudor-style shopping mall, between Lottie's Place, Old Lace Collectibles, and the Lynwood Theater (the island's only movie house). It's a small place with black booths, white walls, Victorian-rose lampshades, a small front room, and a bar. The food is good and they offer a small microbrew menu.

The Harbour Public House

231 Parfitt Way
842-0969
Daily 11 AM-midnight

The Harbour is a very comfortable spot that provides all the amenities the modern consumer wants in a pub or alehouse. It's very beer-conscious, with a dozen brews on tap and a staff that is genial, efficient, and very knowledgeable about the beer. The kitchen offers pub grub with a gourmet twist. The building itself is a remodeled 1881 homestead house. Inside, it's small, but with a spacious feel thanks to the white walls, wood accents, sizable windows, and high ceilings. There's a fireplace area and a spacious deck.

The clientele ranges from the ponytailed men and silver-earringed women who typify the notion of a Bainbridge Islander to Navy officers in uniform who have stopped off on their way back to Bremerton from some official function. The Harbour Pub looks down on the boats and the shimmering water of Eagle Harbor. The masts, the craft moving in and out of the marina, the subtly changing light, and the view that goes all the way across Puget Sound to the Cascades rising in the distance make the setting very satisfying.

Streamliner Diner

397 Winslow Way
842-8595
Daily 8 AM-2:30 PM

Bainbridge Island is just a 30-minute ferry ride

from downtown Seattle, so it doesn't require quite the amount of expedition planning that some ferry trips demand. (If you *are* looking for a more ambitious trip, Bainbridge Island can be a gateway to the Olympic Peninsula.) The Streamliner Diner is a popular little breakfast and lunch storefront right on the quaintly busy main street in the town of Bainbridge (formerly Winslow). It's just a few blocks from the ferry terminal, certainly within walking distance, if you are inclined to walk on in Seattle. The Streamliner has big windows that look out on the tourist-filled streets, chrome chairs with red seats, unmatched tablecloths, and a bright and open feel. The interior is white-and-wood, with tables and counter seating. There's a little front deck for nice weather. The only caveat regarding the Streamliner is its hours: the place closes in the mid-afternoon.

South

KENT

Pony Keg
8535 S 212th St
395-8022
Daily 10 AM-2 AM

The Pony Keg reflects its south-end location, out beyond Longacres racetrack and Sea-Tac Airport, between Highway 167 and the East Valley Highway. There's no neighborhood; the bar is in a strip mall on a busy arterial next to a business park with all kinds of performance-car supply shops. The Pony Keg, with its wood exterior, provides a little respite from all that. It's the kind of place where neon signs for Bud Light and Guinness Extra Stout coexist peacefully in the window, and where Bud and Guinness drinkers coexist peacefully inside. The Pony Keg has 16 beers on tap. The decor is generic Northwest bar: tables arrayed near the front windows, the walls messily adorned with beer and Seahawks posters. Pool tables and video games fill the hinter reaches.

RENTON

Lazy Bee Pub & Eatery

739 Rainier Ave S
255-7423
Sun-Thurs 11 AM-9 PM, Fri & Sat 11AM-11PM

The Lazy Bee, which opened in late 1991 near the Boeing Renton plant, features aeronautical memorabilia, including scale-model planes hanging from the ceiling. The customers include Boeing workers as well as tourists who have visited the nearby Museum of Flight. The pub serves microbrews and a lunch and dinner menu of pizza, gourmet burgers, pasta, sandwiches, soups, salad, fish and chips, plus Thomas Kemper root beer on tap.

TACOMA

Engine House No. 9

611 N Pine St
272-3435
Daily 11 AM-2 AM

Engine House
No. 9 is one of
the more
micro-oriented
drinkeries in
the area. It has
some 20
microbrews or
imports on
tap, plus another couple of dozen in bottles. It also
offers a sampler, which consists of five-ounce glasses
of any three draft beers. E9, as it is called, has a
changing beer menu (including wine and
nonalcoholics) that describes three or four featured
microbrews. The menu might also include a few
paragraphs on something special from the kitchen,
such as the old-world breads served with the soups.
You can even get a "Beer Club" punch card: once you
drink your way through nearly 50 different brews,
your name is engraved on a connoisseurs' plaque.

The Engine House is in a carefully restored old
red-brick firehouse with an outdoor patio. Inside, it's
furnished with old patterned carpets on the wood
floor. There's a lot of old firefighting equipment
around—brass hose ends, ladders, a bell, an old fire
box, some helmets—but not so much that it seems
kitschy. When the afternoon sun streams in through

the windows, the spacious front room is very cozy. The darker back barroom is separated from the dining area by the frames of the old horse stalls, which still have the horses' names above them.

Katie Downs

3211 Ruston Way
756-0771
Sun-Thurs 11 AM-midnight,
Fri & Sat 11 AM-1 AM

Located among a string of bayfront restaurants (C.I. Shenanigans and a new Salty's flank it), Katie Downs is a restaurant with a nice feel and good food. Even more impressive, the restaurant sits over the water and has a panoramic view of the sailboats on Commencement Bay. The restaurant is also near a Tacoma Fire Department station, so you may also see the occasional fireboat out on the water spurting its geysers around. The windows run floor to ceiling, and there is patio seating for the good-weather season. Even on rainy days, the restaurant is fairly bright and airy, thanks in part to the skylights. There are always several local microbrews on tap, plus imports from around the world. You might even see an Australian beer, called Blue Thunder From Down Under, although whether you want to try it is another question.

The world's oldest existing brewery is the Weihenstephan Brewery in Freising, Germany. It was founded in 1040. Old Bushmills of County Antrim, Ireland, claims to have started production in 1608.

The Spar
2121 N 30th St
627-0771
Mon-Sat 11 AM-2 AM, Sun 9 AM-midnight

Located in the Old Town area, just a block up
from Commencement Bay, the Spar is a popular
cafe/bar. It has the classic Northwest pub look of light
wood, well-worn wood floor, cream-colored walls,
and ferryboat-green accents. The room is L-shaped,
with several big tables in the section just inside the
front door. The tables handle six or eight people, so
sometimes two unrelated parties occupy opposite
ends. At mid-room is the bar itself and a pool-table
area with an interesting piece of wall art: a world map
covered with foreign currency that has come in to the
Spar over the years. The back dining area looks out at
the water. There are several micros on tap and a solid
menu of pub grub.

When Beer Meets
FOOD

*S*ince beer has gained cachet as part of a sophisticated lifestyle, it's natural that more attention is also being paid to the beer-food relationship. As Michael Jackson, the dean of beer writers, says, "Beer, like wine, can be a pleasure apart, but all drinks enjoy the company of good food." Cookbook author Jay Harlow echoes the sentiment: "Beer is a refreshing beverage by itself, but it is at its best when accompanied by good foods."

Is there a beer equivalent of "white wine with fish, red wine with meat?" Not really. Most beer connoisseurs agree that richer and heavier meals call for more flavorful and highly hopped beers, and those tend to be darker. But a dark dry stout or porter is also delicious with seafood and with pasta. And poultry can go either way, with a darker beer, a refreshing wheaten, or a pilsner lager.

Beer writer Jack Erickson suggests the following pairings:

Seafood: pilsner, amber lager, spicy ale
Shellfish: porter, stout
Poultry: amber lager, ale
Pork, veal, beef: amber lager, brown ale
Game meat: Scottish ale, porter, dry stout
Roasts and stews: amber lager, porter, stout
Cheese, desserts: pale ale, porter, sweet stout, lambics

These combinations are a good starting point. But Erickson's suggestions may be a bit too timid for many Northwesterners who are ahead of the rest of the country when it comes to culinary ideas. Erickson is basically suggesting lighter beer with lighter food. Feel free to be more adventurous.

In general, rich, full-flavored Northwest ales pair up nicely with seafood, oysters, highly spiced entrées, fowl, game, and cheeses. The wheaten ales are a more appropriate accompaniment to soups, lightly seasoned entrées, and corn-based dishes, such as polenta and corn chowder.

One important point to consider is that the

bitterness of hops, like the tannin in red wine, cuts through the effect of fats on the palate. When you're eating rich foods such as beef, duck, sausages, or cheese, a sip of well-hopped ale can rinse off the fatty film and clear the tastebuds for more. Beer usually goes well with foods that are difficult to match with wine, such as chile-spiked cuisines from tropical and Asian cultures. It also goes well with favored foods of southern Europe and northern Africa, such as olives, garlic, tangy cheeses, and herbs.

Cooking with Beer

There are a number of terrific books on this subject, and there will no doubt be more. Two of the best so far are Jay Harlow's *Beer Cuisine, A Cookbook for Beer Lovers* and *Real Beer & Good Eats: The Rebirth of America's Beer and Food Traditions* by Denis Kelly and Bruce Aidells.

Beer most often adds bitterness (sometimes sweetness) to a recipe, provides flavor and depth, and acts as a carrier for other flavors. Any kind of beer can be used in cooking, but the best choices tend to be the milder varieties with more maltiness and less hop flavor. Some cooks say that the beer should be flat.

Beer isn't alcoholic when used in cooking. As soon as it is heated to about 173° F, the alcohol evaporates, leaving the barley, hops, and yeast to flavor the food. As the water and alcohol evaporate, the flavors become more vivid. A sweet beer gets sweeter, a bitter beer becomes more so. Bitterness is the element to watch most closely. Jay Harlow suggests thinking of beer as a liquid extract of a bitter herb. "Use it with discretion as you would use other assertive herbs," he says.

My own experience is that in sauces, beer seems to retain its beery flavor. A sauce made with dark beer will have a pronounced bitterness and yeastiness. Beer batter for chicken or fish, on the other hand, seems to retain only a light beer taste. And beer used in a heavily spiced dish such as chili tends to be assimilated into the overall taste or overwhelmed by stronger flavors.

There are lots of variations on basic beer batter, to be used with fish or for fruit or vegetable fritters. Beer can also be added to most bread recipes as a substitute for other liquids. And some of the newer beer cookbooks include elaborate, ambitious recipes for such dishes as duck or pheasant braised in ale. Here's a small sampling of recipes.

RECIPES

Classic Beer Cheese

1 pound sharp cheddar cheese, grated
3 garlic cloves, mashed
1 tablespoon Worcestershire sauce
1 teaspoon dry mustard
2 or 3 dashes Tabasco sauce, or to taste
1 cup beer
½ teaspoon salt, or to taste

1. Combine cheese, garlic, Worcestershire sauce,
   mustard, and Tabasco sauce in a food processor
   and blend until smooth. Add beer a little at a time,
   until the mixture is of spreading consistency.
   Add salt to taste.
2. Pack the spread into an airtight container and chill
   thoroughly.
3. Serve at room temperature with pale ale or porter.

Welsh Rarebit

1 tablespoon butter
1 tablespoon flour
1 tablespoon milk
¼ cup brown ale or dark beer
2 teaspoons Worcestershire sauce
1 teaspoon prepared English mustard
½ teaspoon salt
½ teaspoon freshly ground black pepper
2 cups grated cheddar cheese
4 slices toast, buttered and kept hot

1. Place oven rack in the center of the oven. Preheat the broiler to medium high.
2. In a medium-sized saucepan, melt the butter over moderate heat. Remove the pan from the heat and stir in the flour to make a smooth paste. Gradually add the milk, ale or beer, Worcestershire sauce, mustard, salt, and pepper, stirring constantly.
3. Return the pan to low heat and cook, stirring constantly, for 2 to 3 minutes or until the mixture is thick and smooth. Add the cheese and cook, stirring constantly, for another minute or until the cheese has melted.
4. Spoon the mixture over the slices of toast. Put the toast under the broiler for 3 to 4 minutes or until the mixture is golden brown.
5. Transfer the rarebit to individual warmed plates and serve immediately. Serves 4.

Chicken Livers Paprika

2 tablespoons butter
1 pound chicken livers, washed, drained,
   and halved
1 medium-sized onion, chopped
1 teaspoon paprika
1 tablespoon flour
1 cup beer
Juice of ½ lemon
Pepper to taste
2 tablespoons cream

1. Melt butter in a large frying pan. Add livers and
   sauté over medium-high heat about 3 minutes.
   Add onion to livers and sauté until onions are soft.
   Stir in paprika and flour. Add beer gradually, then
   lemon juice. Season with pepper and add cream.
   Simmer for 4 minutes.
2. Serve over toast or rice. Serves 4.

Beer Batter for Chicken, Vegetables, or Fruit

1 cup flour
½ teaspoon paprika
¼ teaspoon baking powder
Pinch of salt
12-ounce bottle of beer
Oil for deep frying
Chicken breasts, vegetables, or fresh fruit

1. Heat oil to 350°–375° F.
2. In medium-sized bowl, combine flour, paprika,

baking powder, and salt. Add beer and gradually blend until frothy. Makes about 2½ cups of batter.

For chicken: Coat several strips of chicken breast with flour, dip in batter, and fry until golden brown, about 8 minutes. Serve with tartar sauce or Chinese duck sauce.

For vegetables: Coat lightly in flour cut-up vegetables such as eggplant strips, zucchini strips, broccoli or cauliflower florets. Dip vegetables in batter and fry about 2 to 5 minutes, depending on thickness.

For fresh fruit: Use bananas cut in half lengthwise, or pears, apples, or peaches sliced into thick rounds. Dip in batter and cook for about 2 to 4 minutes, depending on thickness. (Cook ripe bananas 2 minutes and green bananas 4 minutes.) Fruit can be served with hot chocolate sauce, vanilla pudding, or sugar. (Any of the following can be added to the batter: 1½ teaspoons vanilla extract, ¾ teaspoon almond extract, or 1 tablespoon Grand Marnier, rum, or other liqueur.)

Corn Fritters in Beer Batter

¾ cup all-purpose flour
1 cup beer
8 ounces frozen corn kernels
¼ teaspoon salt
About ½ cup canola or corn oil
Sour cream and caviar for garnish (optional)

1. Place the flour in a mixing bowl. Pour in about
   ¾ cup of the beer and whisk until smooth. Add the
   remainder of the beer and mix again. Place the
   frozen corn in a sieve and run it under warm tap
   water to defrost. Drain well and add to the batter,
   along with the salt.
2. Heat 1½ to 2 tablespoons of the oil in each of two
   large skillets. When the oil is hot, spoon about 1½
   tablespoons of the batter into each skillet and
   spread it out with a spoon. (Don't be concerned
   about a few holes here and there.) Spoon in more
   batter to make three or four fritters at a time in
   each skillet, spreading the batter out for each
   fritter. Cook about 3 minutes per side, until brown
   and crisp, then transfer to a wire rack. Add oil to
   the skillets as needed.
3. Serve the fritters immediately, or reheat them later
   in a hot oven or under a broiler. Top with sour
   cream and caviar if desired. Serves 6.

Beer and Onion Soup

3 pounds onions (8 to 10 medium-sized), peeled
   and sliced
2 to 3 garlic cloves, minced
¾ cup butter
2 cups vegetable broth
2½ cups dark beer or stout
1¼ cups cream
2 teaspoons salt
2 teaspoons paprika
Dash of Tabasco sauce
Fresh-ground black pepper to taste
2 to 4 teaspoons sugar (depending on the
   bitterness of the beer)
2 teaspoons cider vinegar
4 egg yolks
Optional garnish: hot paprika, or toasted croutons
   and grated Parmesan cheese

1. Slowly cook the onions and garlic in the butter until the onions are transparent and soft.
2. Add the vegetable broth. Purée the mixture in a blender or food processor in batches of 2 or 3 cups.
3. Pour the purée into a large pot and add the beer, cream, salt, paprika, Tabasco, pepper, sugar, and vinegar. Simmer, stirring often, for about 20 minutes.
4. Beat the egg yolks with a whisk. Continue beating them while adding a small amount of the hot soup to the egg yolks.
5. Pour the egg yolk mixture into the pot of soup and whisk quickly. Cook the soup a few minutes more over very low heat, stirring constantly. It should be slightly thickened.
6. Serve the soup very hot, sprinkled with a little hot paprika or garnish with the croutons and Parmesan cheese. Serves 6 to 8.

Tillamook Cheddar-Beer Soup

¼ cup butter
1½ cups chopped yellow onion
1 cup peeled and sliced carrots
1 cup chopped celery
2 cups diced new potatoes
2 cups chicken broth
½ cup flour
2 cups milk
3 cups grated cheddar cheese
1 tablespoon dry mustard
⅛ teaspoon cayenne pepper
½ bottle beer (6 ounces)

1. Melt the butter in a heavy 6-quart saucepan. Add vegetables and sauté briefly. Pour in the chicken broth and simmer for 30 minutes.
2. Mix flour and milk together until smooth, then blend into soup. Stir and cook until well blended. Add cheese, mustard, and cayenne.
3. Stir until cheese melts, then stir in beer. Serves 6.

Trout in Beer

3 fresh trout
1 cup beer
1 cup dry white wine
½ cup vinegar
Juice of 1 lemon
Lemon slices and parsley for garnish

1. Place cleaned trout in a skillet. Mix beer, wine, and vinegar and pour over the fish.
2. Bring the mixture to a boil, then reduce the heat and simmer for 10 to 15 minutes, turning fish once.
3. Remove the fish to a platter and squeeze fresh lemon juice over them. Garnish with lemon slices and parsley.

Carp Baked in Beer

6 tablespoons butter
1 cup sliced onions
½ cup diced celery
3 pounds dressed carp
Salt and ground black pepper
1 cup light ale or beer
2 stalks parsley
2 tablespoons gingerbread or gingersnap crumbs
Carp roe
1 teaspoon lemon juice
Parsley for garnish

1. Preheat oven to 325° F.
2. Melt 2 tablespoons of the butter in a baking dish. Add onion and celery and mix well. Rub fish lightly with salt and pepper and lay over vegetables. Add beer and parsley. Sprinkle gingerbread or gingersnap crumbs over the top.
3. Cover and cook in oven at 325° F for 30 to 40 minutes, or until the fish flakes when tested with a fork. Transfer fish to a warmed platter and keep it warm. Reserve the stock.
4. In a saucepan over high heat, reduce the stock by one-half, then strain.
5. Meanwhile, slice the carp roe, sprinkle lightly with salt, pepper, and lemon juice, and cook in 2 tablespoons of butter over low heat for 5 minutes or until done.
6. Arrange the roe around the fish. Add remaining 2 tablespoons of butter to the reduced stock, heat, adjust seasonings, and pour over the fish. Garnish with parsley. Serves 6.

Beer-Steamed Clams

16 to 24 small, live clams (1 to 1½ pounds total)
½ bottle beer (6 ounces)
6 to 8 slices fresh ginger
2 green onions or shallots, sliced
1½ tablespoons unsalted butter
French bread

1. Scrub the clams well, discarding any open ones that do not close when handled.
2. Place the clams in a saucepan with the beer, ginger, and green onions or shallots. Cover, bring to a boil, and cook until most of the shells are open, 3 to 5 minutes.
3. Transfer the open clams to a serving bowl and cook the remaining clams another minute or two. Discard the ones that do not open.
4. Swirl the butter into the broth and pour the broth over the clams.
5. Serve with crusty bread for dunking. Serves 2.

Beer Batter Fish

1 cup flour
1 teaspoon baking powder
1 egg, beaten
2 tablespoons vegetable oil
1 cup light beer
Peanut oil for deep-frying
1½ pounds ling cod fillets, cut into 2-inch pieces
Tartar sauce
Lemon wedges

1. Whisk together flour, baking powder, egg, vegetable oil, and beer.
2. Heat peanut oil to 375° F.
3. Coat fish with batter and drop 2 to 3 pieces at a time into the oil. Fry until golden brown, turning once.
4. Drain well on paper towels. Serve with tartar sauce and lemon wedges. Serves 2.

Sweet Potatoes Congolese

2 cups flour
2 cups beer
4 medium-sized sweet potatoes
¼ cup honey
¼ cup brandy
1 teaspoon grated lemon peel
Fat for deep-frying

1. Blend the flour and the beer into a smooth batter.
   Set aside.
2. Blanch the whole sweet potatoes for 5 minutes in
   boiling water, then peel and slice them. Marinate
   for 1 hour in the honey, brandy, and lemon peel.
3. Without drying the slices, dip them in the batter.
   Fry them in fat heated to 390° F until golden
   brown.
4. Serve very hot. These fritters are excellent with
   roast turkey. Serves 4.

Beer Bread (Øllebröd)
(Makes 1 large loaf or 3 small loaves)

2 cups tepid water
1½ cups beer
⅔ cup molasses, warmed to tepid
2 quarter-ounce packages active dry yeast
5 cups rye flour
5 cups all-purpose flour
2 teaspoons salt

1. Mix 1½ cups of the tepid water with the beer and molasses. Mix the yeast with the remaining ½ cup of water, then add to the beer mixture. Add the rye and all-purpose flours and the salt. Mix well.
2. Let the dough rise in a warm place until doubled in bulk, about 1½ hours.
3. Knead on a floured board, using additional all-purpose flour, if necessary, to make a stiff dough—about 10 minutes.
4. To make one large loaf, place the dough in a floured cloth in a large bowl and let it rise again until doubled in bulk. For three loaves, divide the dough into three equal parts and let them rise separately. After it has risen, turn the dough upside down into one large, buttered loaf pan or three smaller loaf pans.
5. Bake the single loaf in a preheated 400° F oven for 10 minutes, then at 325° F for 50 minutes. Bake three small loaves for 10 minutes at 400° F, then at 325° F for 35 to 40 minutes.

Chicken in Beer

4 tablespoons butter
2½- to 3-pound chicken, trussed
Salt and pepper
1 tablespoon chopped shallots
½ cup gin
1 cup heavy cream
½ pound fresh mushrooms, diced (2½ cups)
2 cups dark beer
Cayenne pepper
2 tablespoons chopped fresh parsley

1. Melt 2 tablespoons of the butter in a fireproof casserole over moderate heat and cook the chicken, turning it, until golden. Add salt and pepper. Cover and cook for 30 minutes over low heat. Remove the chicken to a heated dish and keep it covered in a warm place.

2. In the same casserole, cook the shallots until golden. Put the chicken back in, pour the gin over it, and flame the gin. Add 1 tablespoon of butter, 2 tablespoons of the cream, and the mushrooms. Pour in the beer and season with salt, pepper, and a little cayenne. Cover and simmer for 15 minutes.

3. When the chicken is done, transfer it to a chopping board and cut into four pieces. Transfer it to a serving dish and keep it covered in a warm place.

4. Pour the rest of the cream into the casserole and boil vigorously for several minutes to thicken the liquid. Adjust the seasoning if necessary.

5. Remove the casserole from the heat and add the rest of the butter. Let it melt in the sauce, then pour the sauce over the chicken.

6. Sprinkle with chopped parsley and serve hot.
   Serves 4.

Dark Beer Sabayon

4 egg yolks
2 tablespoons sugar
¾ teaspoon lemon juice
¼ cup dark beer
¼ cup whipped cream (measured after whipping)

1. Beat the egg yolks, sugar, and lemon juice with a
   wire whisk in an unlined, round-bottom copper
   basin or metal bowl. Put the basin or bowl over
   gentle heat (you may set it in a water bath) and
   beat rapidly while adding the beer. Beat vigorously
   until the sauce is about four or five times its
   original volume.
2. Set the basin or bowl on a bed of ice cubes and
   continue beating until cold. Fold in the whipped
   cream. This beer sabayon can be eaten by itself, or
   spooned over another dessert, such as gingerbread
   pudding. Serves 8.

BEER BEVERAGES

Generally speaking, beer is pretty good by itself, without anything to dress it up. But sometimes a slice of lemon can enhance a wheat beer. A "fox" made of beer and a dash of lime juice can also be quite intriguing. And since brewers themselves often play around with various ingredients, ranging from fruits to chile peppers, there's no reason why beer drinkers shouldn't get creative, too. You'll want to try an old recipe for Beer Syllabub, since surely most of our readers will have a milk cow handy, as the recipe requires.

Ale Flip

In a shaker, mix a pint of ale with crushed ice and one egg.

Beer Syllabub

This is a fun drink to prepare for summer country house guests. Making it can be a great sharpshooting contest for the crowd.

Get ready a handful of dried currants, which have been washed and allowed to swell up nice and plump in boiling water, then seed them. Into a large punch bowl, put 1 pint of beer and the same quantity of hard cider—light beer and good bottled cider. Sweeten to taste with sugar, add currants and a dash or so of nutmeg. Now have your cow set and ready—able and willing—and the expert milker on the job. Hold the bowl at a safe and convenient distance from the cow and milk directly into the bowl about three pints of milk.

Milk infused in this way is creamy and frothy and the syllabub is a picturesque drink.

Burton Soda

Mix together equal parts ale and ginger beer.

Island Grog

Heat 12 ounces of pilsner with four coffeespoons of powdered sugar and one soupspoon of white rum. Remove from heat just before boiling and serve hot.

Shandygaff

Mix together equal parts well-chilled light beer and ginger ale. This is a popular summer drink in India, Asia, and England.

Waldorf Beer Flip

Pour 3 pints of beer into a saucepan. Add 1 tablespoon of sugar, the grated rind of half a small lemon (or still better, the rind cut into small pieces), a pinch of mace, 1 whole clove, head removed, and ½ teaspoon of sweet butter. Bring to a boil and remove from the heat. Strain the mixture. Beat the white of 1 egg and yolks of 2 eggs with 2 tablespoons of beer, and gradually stir briskly into the hot beer mixture. Beat with electric mixer until frothy. Serve in heated punch cups. Serves 6.

Wassail Beer Bowl

Heat three quarts of beer, but not to boiling. Pour off and set aside two quarts of the beer. To the remaining quart, add 1 pound of powdered sugar, a freshly grated whole nutmeg, ½ teaspoon of powdered ginger, 1 cup of sherry wine, and the other two quarts of hot beer with 4 or 5 thin slices of seeded lemon. Bring almost to boiling point; the surface will look pearly. Remove from heat. Taste for sweetening, and pour into a large heated bowl containing 6 slices of freshly made toast. Serve as hot as possible in punch glasses. Serves 16-18.

Other Regional
BREWPUBS
and Microbreweries

*B*rewpubs are popping up all over the country now, but the West Coast remains the most active area. From Alaska and British Columbia to southern California, the beer connoisseur has plenty of quaffing options.

Oregon

B. Moloch Bakery & Pub
901 SW Salmon St
Portland, OR 97205
(503) 227-5700
(Brewpub and microbrewery)

Bay Front Brewery and Public House
748 Bay Blvd
Newport, OR 97365
(503) 265-3188

Bridgeport Brewpub
1313 NW Marshall St
Portland, OR 97209
(503) 241-7179

Cornelius Pass Roadhouse
Route 5, Box 340
Cornelius Pass Rd, just south
of Hwy 26
Hillsboro, OR 97124
(503) 640-6174

Deschutes Brewery & Public House
1044 NW Bond St
Bend, OR 97701
(503) 382-9242

Fulton Pub & Brewery
618 SW Nebraska St
Portland, OR 97201
(503) 246-9530

Highland Pub & Brewery
4225 SE 182nd Ave
Gresham, OR 97030
(503) 665-3015

Highstreet Pub & Brewery
1243 High St
Eugene, OR 97401
(503) 345-4905

Hillsdale Brewery & Public House
1505 SW Sunset Blvd
Portland, OR 97201
(503) 246-3938

Hood River Brewing Co.
506 Columbia St
Hood River, OR 97031
(503) 386-2281
(Brewpub and microbrewery)

Lighthouse Brewpub
4157 N Hwy 101
Lincoln City, OR 97367
(503) 994-7238

McMenamins
6179 SW Murray Blvd
Beaverton, OR 97005
(503) 644-4562

Old World Deli
341 SW Second St
Corvallis, OR 97333
(503) 752-8549

Oregon Trail Brewery
341 SW Second St
Corvallis, OR 97333
(503) 758-3527

The Pizza Deli & Brewery
249 N Redwood Hwy
Cave Junction, OR 97523
(503) 592-3556

Portland Brewing Co.
1339 NW Flanders
Portland, OR 97209
(503) 222-7150
(Brewpub and microbrewery)

Roger's Zoo
2037 Sherman
North Bend, OR 97459
(503) 756-1463

Rogue Brewing Co. & Public House
31B Water St
Ashland, OR 97520
(503) 488-5061

Steelhead Brewery
Fifth and Pearl
Eugene, OR 97401
(503) 686-BREW

WhiteCap Brew Pub
506 Columbia St
Hood River, OR 97031
(503) 386-2247

Widmer Brewing Co.
929 N Russel St
or 923 SW Ninth St
Portland, OR 97227
(503) 281-BIER

Idaho

Coeur d'Alene Brewing Co.
204 N Second St
Coeur d'Alene, ID 83814
(208) 664-BREW

Harrison Hollow Brewhouse
2455 Harrison Hollow St
Boise, ID 83702
(208) 343-6820

Table Rock Brewpub
705 Fulton St
Boise, ID 83702
(208) 342-0944

Alaska

Alaskan Brewing & Bottling
5429 Shaune Dr
Juneau, AK 99801
(907) 780-4514

Yukon Brewery
7851 Spring St
Anchorage, AK 99518
(907) 349-7191

British Columbia

Granville Island Brewing Co.
1441 Cartwright St, Granville Island
Vancouver, BC V6H 3R7
(604) 688-9927

Horseshoe Bay Brewery
6695 Nelson Ave
West Vancouver, BC V7W 2B2
(604) 921-6116

Island Pacific/Vancouver Island Brewing
6809 Kirkpatrick Crescent, RR#3
Victoria, BC V8X 3X1
(604) 652-4722

Leeward Neighbourhood Brewpub
649 Anderton Rd
Comox, BC V9N 5B7
(604) 339-5400

Okanagan Spring
2801 27A Ave
Vernon, BC V1T 1T5
(604) 433-0088

Prairie Inn Cottage Brewpub
7806 E Saanich Rd
Saanichan, BC V5L 5B2
(604) 255-4550

Shaftebury Brewing
1973 Pandora Dr
Vancouver, BC V7G 1V2
(604) 255-4550

Spinnakers Brewpub
308 Catherine St
Victoria, BC V9A 3S8
(604) 382-5199

Swan's Brewpub/Buckerfield's Brewery
506 Pandora
Victoria, BC V8W 1N6
(604) 361-3310

California

Alpine Village Brewing
833 W Torrance Blvd
Torrance, CA 90502
(213) 329-8881
(Microbrewery)

Anchor Brewing Co.
1705 Mariposa St
San Francisco, CA 94107
(415) 863-8350
(Microbrewery)

Angeles Brewing Co.
10009 Canoga Ave
Chatsworth, CA 91311
(818) 407-0340

Bison Brewing Co.
2598 Telegraph Ave
Berkeley, CA 94704
(415) 841-7734

Brewpub on the Green
3400 Stevenson Blvd
Fremont, CA 94538
(415) 651-5510

Buckhorn Saloon/Anderson Valley Brewing Co.
14081 Hwy 128
Boonville, CA 95415
(707) 895-BEER

Buffalo Bill's Brew Pub
1082 B St
Hayward, CA 94541
(415) 886-9823

Butterfield Brewery
777 E Olive Ave
Fresno, CA 93728
(209) 264-5521

Crown City Brewery
300 S Raymond Ave
Pasadena, CA 91105
(818) 577-5548

Dead Cat Alley Brewing
666 Dead Cat Alley
Woodland, CA 95695
(916) 661-1521

Emery Pub
5800 Shellmound Ave
Emeryville, CA 94608
(510) 653-0444

Gordon-Biersch Brewing Co.
640 Emerson St
Palo Alto, CA 94301
(415) 323-7723

Gorky's Russian Brewery
536 E 8th
Los Angeles, CA 90014
(213) 463-4060

Grapevine Brewery & Pub
658 Lebec Rd
Lebec, CA 93243
(805) 248-6890

Hogshead Brewing Co.
114 J St
Sacramento, CA 95814
(916) 443-BREW

Humboldt Brewing Co.
856 10th St
Arcata, CA 95521
(707) 826-BREW

**Karl Strauss Old Columbia
Brewery & Grill**
1157 Columbia St
San Diego, CA 92101
(619) 234-BREW

Kelmer's Brewhouse
458 B St
Santa Rosa, CA 95401
(707) 544-HOPS

Lind Brewing Co.
1933 Davis St #177
San Leandro, CA 94577
(415) 562-0866
(Microbrewery)

Los Angeles Brewing Co.
1845 S Bundy Dr
Los Angeles, CA 90025
(213) 207-1000
(Microbrewery)

Mammoth Lakes Brewing
170 Mountain Blvd
Mammoth Lakes, CA 93546
(619) 934-8134

Marin Brewing Co.
1809 Larkspur Landing Circle
Larkspur, CA 94939
(415) 461-4677

Mendocino Brewing Co.
13351 S Hwy 101
Hopland, CA 95449
(707) 744-1015

Mission Brewing Co.
1751 Hancock St
San Diego, CA 92110
(619) 294-3363

Monterey Brewing Co.
638 Wave St
Monterey, CA 93940
(408) 375-3634

**Napa Valley Brewing Co./
Calistoga Inn**
1250 Lincoln Ave
Calistoga, CA 94515
(707) 942-4101

Nevada City Brewing
75 Bost Ave
Nevada City, CA 95959
(916) 265-2446
(Microbrewery)

North Coast Brewing Co.
444 N Main St
Fort Bragg, CA 95420
(707) 964-2739

Pacific Coast Brewing
906 Washington St
Oakland, CA 94607
(415) 836-2739

Rubicon Brewing Co.
2004 Capitol Ave
Sacramento, CA 95814
(916) 448-7032

San Andreas Brewing
737 San Benito
Hollister, CA 95023
(408) 637-7074

San Francisco Brewing Co.
155 Columbus Ave
San Francisco, CA 94133
(415) 434-3344

Santa Cruz Brewing Co.
516 Front St
Santa Cruz, CA 95060
(408) 429-8838 or 429-8915

**Seabright Brewery Pub &
Restaurant**
519 Seabright Ave
Santa Cruz, CA 95062
(408) 426-BREW

Sierra Nevada Brewing Co.
1075 E 20th St
Chico, CA 95928
(916) 893-3520
(Microbrewery)

SLO Brewing
1119 Garden St
San Luis Obispo, CA 93401
(805) 543-1843

Stanislaus Brewing Co.
3454 Shoemaker Ave
Modesto, CA 95351
(209) 523-2262
(Microbrewery)

**Tied House Restaurant &
Brewery**
954 Villa St
Mountain View, CA
94041
(415) 965-BREW

Truckee Brewing Co.
11401 Donner Pass Rd
Truckee, CA 95734
(916) 587-7411

Willette's Brewery
902 Main St
Napa, CA 94559
(707) 258-BEER

Winchester Brewing Co.
820 Winchester Blvd S
San Jose, CA 95128
(408) 243-7561

Organizations, Publications, and Events

Organizations

Association of Brewers
PO Box 287
Boulder, CO 80306

Bar Tourists of America
c/o Jack McDougall
12 Sylvester St
Cranford, NJ 07016

Institute for Brewing Studies
PO Box 1679
Boulder, CO 80306-1679

Microbrew Appreciation Society
12345 Lake City Way NE #159
Seattle, WA 98125
365-5812

Publications

American Brewer Magazine
PO Box 510
Hayward, CA 94541
(415) 538-9500

Beer Enthusiast
(a catalog of books, T-shirts, etc.)
c/o Institute for Brewing Studies
PO Box 1679
Boulder, CO 80306-1679

Celebrator Beer News
PO Box 375
Hayward, CA 94543

The Moderation Reader
c/o Gene Ford Publications
4714 NE 50th St
Seattle, WA 98105-2908

The Northwest Beer Journal
2677 Fircrest Dr SE
Port Orchard, WA 98366
(206) 871-1692

The Pint Post
c/o Microbrew Appreciation Society
12345 Lake City Way NE #159
Seattle, WA 98125
(206) 365-5812

World Beer Review
WBR Publications
PO Box 71
Clemson, SC 29633

Zymurgy
(The Magazine for Homebrewers and
Beer Lovers)
PO Box 287
Boulder, CO 80306-0827

Events

Great American Beer Festival
October in Denver
Organized by the Association of
Brewers
PO Box 287
Boulder, CO 80306

The Great British Beer Tour
& Ultimate Pub Crawl
c/o Ciao! Travel
2707 Congress St, Suite 1F
San Diego, CA 92110
(619) 297-8112
1-800-942-2426

Great Northwest Beer Festival
September at F.X. McCrory's in
Seattle

The Great Northwest
Microbrewery Invitational
Mid- to late-September at the
Seattle Center
Most of the Northwest's brewers
have booths and serve samples.

Northwest Ale Festival
Mid-September at Cooper's Alehouse
in Seattle
Organized by the Microbrew
Appreciation Society
12345 Lake City Way NE #159
Seattle, WA 98125
365-5812

Oregon Brewer's Festival
Third weekend in July

More Reading About Brews

Forget, Carl, comp. *The Association of Brewers' Dictionary of Beer and Brewing.* Boulder, Colorado: Brewers Publications, 1988.

Harlow, Jay. *Beer Cuisine: A Cookbook for Beer Lovers.* Emeryville, California: Harlow & Ratner, 1991.

Jackson, Michael. *New World Guide to Beer.* Philadelphia: Running Press, 1988.

————. *Pocket Guide to Beer.* New York: Simon & Schuster, 1991.

Anderson, Will. *Beer USA.* Dobbs Ferry, New York: Morgan & Morgan, 1986.

Erickson, Jack. *Brewery Adventures in the Wild West.* Reston, Virginia: Red Brick Press, 1991.

————. *Great Cooking With Beer.* Reston, Virginia: Red Brick Press, 1989.

Finch, Christopher. *A Connoisseur's Guide to the World's Best Beer.* New York: Abbeville Press, 1989.

Kelly, Denis, and Bruce Aidells. *Real Beer & Good Eats: The Rebirth of America's Beer and Food Traditions.* New York: Knopf, 1992.

Meier, Gary, and Gloria Meier. *Brewed in the Pacific Northwest.* Seattle: Fjord Press, 1991.

Robertson, James D. *The Connoisseur's Guide to Beer.* Ottawa, Illinois: Jameson Books, 1984.

Index

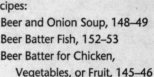

ALASKA NORTHWEST BOOKS™
proudly recommends more of its books on Northwest lifestyle:

Seattle Emergency Espresso: The Insider's Guide to Neighborhood Coffee Spots, by Heather Doran Barbieri.
Seattle, America's premier espresso city, now has its own guide to finding the ultimate coffee fix. Arranged by neighborhood, this guide takes you to more than 100 espresso carts, coffeehouses, cafes, and restaurants in the greater Seattle area. Brief sections are included on the history of the local coffee scene and the major roasting companies, as well as tips on knowing coffees and the language of espresso. With illustrations, 1 map.
Softbound, 180 pages, $9.95, ISBN 0-88240-399-0

Caprial's Seasonal Kitchen: An Innovative Chef's Menus and Recipes for Easy Home Cooking, by Caprial Pence.
In her exciting first cookbook, award-winning Northwest chef Caprial Pence invites the home cook to discover the secrets of her innovative style. Her delectable menus with 116 recipes that use the freshest seasonal ingredients are perfect for satisfying family and friends. With 44 illustrations.
Softbound, 340 pages, $12.95, ISBN 0-88240-418-0;
hardbound, $19.95, ISBN 0-88240-417-2

Seattle Picnics: Favorite Sites, Seasonal Menus, and 100 Recipes, by Barbara Holz Sullivan.
Seattle Picnics is a guide to more than 40 favorite Seattle-area picnic sites, with theme picnic menus, organized by season, and 100 special recipes. Besides advice on where to go, how to get there, and how to prepare original picnic fare, there's also a handy guide to selected take-out food locations for instant picnics. With a map.
Softbound, 304 pages, $10.95, ISBN 0-88240-408-3

Many other fascinating books are available from Alaska Northwest Books™. Ask at your favorite bookstore or write us for a free catalog.

Alaska Northwest Books™
A division of GTE Discovery Publications, Inc.
P.O. Box 3007, Bothell, WA 98040-3007
1-800-343-4567